LEADER'S GUIDE (Youth Edition)
Course One: *12 Truths to Nourish Your Soul*

Opportunity Makers

24 Seeds for a Fruitful Future

Evan Keller

with Candice Davis & Jeff Hostetter

Creating Jobs Inc
DeLand FL

Opportunity Makers: 24 Seeds for a Fruitful Future
Course One Leaders Guide: 12 Truths to Nourish Your Soul

Copyright © 2021 by Creating Jobs Inc

All rights reserved. No parts of this book may be reproduced in any form without written permission from Creating Jobs Inc.

Published by:
Creating Jobs Inc
1702 N Woodland Blvd #116437
DeLand, FL 32720
World Wide Web: www.creatingjobs.org
E-mail: info@creatingjobs.org

Scripture taken from the International Children's Bible®. Copyright © 1986, 1988, 1999 by Thomas Nelson. Used by permission. All rights reserved.

ISBN 978-1-7355656-6-8

Printed in the United States of America

Dedication

Opportunity Makers is dedicated to World Vision and Compassion International, whose staff and volunteers daily nurture "fruitful futures" in young people around the world, and to their Honduran leaders who were the catalyst for this curriculum.

Contents

Introduction 1

Lessons

   A. Introducing Opportunity Makers 5

   B. Introducing Identity and Purpose 9

   C. Introducing the Life of Joseph 13

   1. Who I Am: Defined by God 17

   2. Who I Am: Cherished Child 25

   3. Who I Am: Healed Relationships 31

   4. Who I Am: Pain that Matures 37

   5. Who I Am: Reflecting God 45

   6. Why I'm Here: God's Plan 53

   7. Why I'm Here: God's Gifts 61

   8. Why I'm Here: Good Work 67

   9. Why I'm Here: Trusting God 75

   10. Why I'm Here: Shaping the Future 83

   11. Why I'm Here: Teamwork 91

   12. Why I'm Here: Generosity 97

   D. Summarizing Identity and Purpose 105

Appendix 109

   Opportunity Makers Overview 111

   Identity Statement 121

   Purpose Statement 125

   Truths At-a-Glance 129

   Truths and 12 Lies12 Lies 133

   Supporting Scriptures for 12 Truths 139

   How Joseph Embodied the 12 Truths 157

   Timeline of Joseph's Life 165

   Truth Lesson Outline 169

   How the 12 Truths Nourished Your Soul 175

   Image of the Moon 179

   Image of Grape Vine with Fruit 183

Image of Birds Flying in a "V" Formation 187

Image of Wall Sitting 191

Bicycle Assembly Diagram 195

Bicycle Assembly Instructions 199

Virtuous Circles Diagram 203

Presentation Feedback Form 207

Contributors 211

Introduction

A Unique Opportunity for Transformation. Coupled with your loving investment in your students, we believe this course bursts with unlimited potential to transform lives. And not because *we* wrote it. God's Word is the key to altering the entire trajectory of your students' lives and families. Joseph's life at the end of Genesis has long been held up as a key example of trusting God amidst trials and embodying character and cooperation with God which points to Jesus. Instead of breezing over these truths or merely laying them out in a short article, we help you create a series of experiences and discussions in which youth (and adults in a forthcoming edition) can absorb and begin to emulate the truths that Joseph embodied so beautifully. We'll help you patiently mine the riches of Joseph's life to illuminate each glorious facet of his surprising, difficult, and godly example.

Patiently Planting Truth Brings Change. While Opportunity Makers may be a longer-than-average course, real change takes time. When soaking in the truth of God's Word as in a long, hot bath, it's goodness begins to permeate the soul. Course One experiences 12 truths that Joseph embodied: five that focus on identity ("who am I") and seven that focus on purpose ("why I'm here"). We believe that embracing these truths and resisting their corresponding lies will firmly plant the seeds of a biblical mindset. You have the crucial role of planting and watering these precious seeds that God can grow into amazing fruit to bless entire families and communities. Thank you for making this priceless investment!

Active and Interactive Learning. After three introductory lessons, each lesson slows down to focus on a single truth, exploring it through both action and imagination exercises. You'll help them enter the story of Joseph and wrestle with how they would respond to different scenarios that he encountered. We provide you with vivid illustrations to help students understand each truth, and Scriptures that reinforce its importance in their lives. Each lesson shows how Jesus is the ultimate model of living the truth. We provide you with a balance of lecture notes and discussion questions so you can both explain truth and help them wrestle with it themselves.

Lesson Format. Each of the 12 truth lessons follows the same outline (see "Truth Lesson Outline" in the Appendix) to give your class a familiar rhythm of learning. If you flip over to an actual lesson, you'll see that we speak *to you* within brackets while the content outside the brackets is for you to speak *to your class*. Bracketed content helps you know what to *do* while unbracketed content helps you know what to *say*. We trust that this Leader's Guide will make it easy to teach this course.

Supporting Materials. Since (unlike Course Two) there is no student handbook for Course One, it is essential that each student has a laminated copy of the "Course One Overview" and brings it to class to refer to during each lesson. Please work with your organizational leaders on a plan to print and laminate this four-page overview (best presented on a single 11x17 sheet if available) found in the Appendix. The Appendix has other tools to assist in your teaching, including a couple of handouts to give to your students and illustrative images to show them. It contains charts and scriptures related to the 12 Truths, including a Genesis manuscript of Joseph's story from the International Children's Bible, the English translation used throughout Opportunity Makers.

Classroom Supplies. In addition to a quiet (if possible) classroom with a whiteboard (and its markers), please provide the following for each student during each lesson: desk, Bible, paper and pencil or pen. When a lesson requires additional supplies, they will be listed at the beginning of the lesson.

Teaching Assistants. If available, have an adult present for every 8-10 students. Your adult assistants can help manage behavior and keep students on track when they are split into smaller groups. Both adults and students (with bold and enthusiastic voices) can read Scriptures to the class during the lessons.

Time. The introductory and summary lessons can be done in 45-60 minutes. The 12 Truths lessons contain roughly 90 minutes of material, so are split into two halves with a break in between. If necessary, the two halves can be done on different days. This time frame can expand or contract depending on how long you allow for discussion of the previous lesson's homework and of the current lesson's questions.

Accountability Partners. We strongly recommend that you pair up each student with an accountability partner. Please work with your organizational leaders to decide how accountability partners will be assigned, how often they will meet, and what parameters you'd like to provide for their meetings in between lessons. We recommend:
- Pair students of the same gender together.
- If they do not live near each other, they can plan to meet in the classroom right after each lesson. But ideally, they will meet midway between lessons to review progress on their homework and pray for each other.
- Pairs meet at least once in between lessons and at least once every other week.

The goal is that having to share with a partner will motivate students to do their homework. These pairs can also provide some of the emotional and spiritual support needed to sustain the deep change in beliefs that we seek. If you can engage parents to further reinforce the homework assignments, that will be powerful.

Putting Truth on the Schedule. Circling back to our mutual goal of transforming your students' lives through God's Word, remember that Jesus said: "blessed are those who hear and *put into practice* these words of mine" (Luke 11:28). With applying Scripture in mind, let's briefly consider another aspect of God's truth: science. Recent brain studies show that forming new habits is a powerful key to sustaining change. When you do something new for at least 21 days, it has a good chance of remaining a regular part of your daily routine. Because they fill our days, those daily rhythms profoundly shape the kind of people we are becoming. Do you see how potent this combination is? When we intentionally apply biblical truth to our Creator's design for habits to profoundly shape us, this uniquely potent combination nurtures slow but lasting change.

A Course that Turns Truths into Habits. Course Two of Opportunity Makers does exactly that. Entitled "12 Habits to Co-Create with God", it will help your students to integrate Course One's biblical identity and purpose into their daily lives. Building on the 12 truths, it offers 12 habits that will help them shape the future with God. Joseph's life is again the prime example, showing how each of the 12 habits is lived out in flesh and blood. Even more practical than Course One, it gives clear and simple guidance for planting and sustaining the habits in students' real lives.

Selective Enrollment for a Demanding Course. Since that's asking a lot, Course Two may not be for everyone. The commitment is much higher than in Course One. The majority of student work will be in between classes rather than in the classroom – including both journaling in their student handbooks and taking action to implement the 12 habits. In fact, it will ask them to change how they spend their time every single day! Since such change will take serious effect, we offer an application process for you to discern who is really serious about living out the 12 truths of Course One through the 12 habits of Course Two. (Read what the 12 habits are on the "12 Habits Bookmark" in the Appendix.)

Sharpening Your Teaching Tools. Another key to transforming your students is communicating effectively. It is not easy or automatic to transfer information from these pages (and from your mind) into distracted young minds of youth is not easy or automatic. It's both art and science. And we rely on God's Spirit to turn information into transformation. To catalyze real change, truth must be experienced as well as acknowledged. So, we've created a course to help you and your teaching assistants to engage the full attention and enthusiasm of your classes.

Our course for trainers and facilitators is entitled "Engage: Communicating for Change" and is available to all Creating Jobs Inc partners. While some of its resources are available to download from CreatingJobs.org, we encourage you to go through the course online or better yet: via Zoom or in-person alongside other teachers in your organization. If you teach Opportunity Makers before taking the communications course, we ask that at the very least you use its primary tool, the "Presentation Feedback Form," which you can find in the Appendix. Please use it to both prepare before teaching a lesson and to get feedback from your adult assistants. If you teach with a team, please print copies of the Presentation Feedback Form to give and receive feedback after each lesson. This will help your team continually sharpen its teaching excellence. This will give your students a double benefit: a strong Joseph-like example of maximizing your gifts as well as communicating in a way that transforms. May God's Spirit fill you and give you the incomparable joy of co-working with Him in the lives of your students!

A. Introducing Opportunity Makers

Requirements.
- **Time.** The lessons contain roughly 60 minutes of material.
- **Supplies.** See Introduction for general supplies needed for every lesson, plus laminated copies of "Course 1 Overview" from the Appendix for each student.
- **Prior Planning.** Decide how accountability partners will be assigned, how often they will meet, and what parameters you'd like to provide for their meetings in between lessons. Recommendations: Pair students of the same gender together. If they do not live near each other, they can plan to meet in the classroom right after each lesson. But ideally, thy will meet midway between lessons to review progress on their homework and pray for each other. They should meet at least once in between lessons and at least once every other week.

Opening Prayer. [Pray]

How do your beliefs about God and yourself shape your life? [Discuss.]

Elephants are much loved for being both tender and fierce, for being powerful and intelligent. They are among the hugest and most unique creatures. They are meant to roam the wilderness, enjoying their freedom and their family. They glorify God by being what He created them to be in relationship to each other and God's earth. But we humans have tried to capture that beauty and make elephants mere performers for our entertainment in circuses. While this vastly reduces the opportunities elephants have to live a full life as God intended, the human method of controlling these massive creatures teaches us an important lesson.

When a circus elephant is very young, a shackle is put on one of its front legs. A small chain connects the shackle to a small peg that is driven into the ground. At first it resists, yanking with all its puny strength until it realizes it can't break free. It gives up. Without enough strength to pull the peg out of the ground, it settles for only walking in a small circle based on the length of the chain. This behavior – having its freedom restricted by a small chain pegged to the ground – becomes normal to the young elephant. Instead of ranging freely with his family in a vast forest, this tiny radius becomes its life. But baby elephants don't stay small. As they eat massive amounts of food, they grow quickly from cute to lumbering. Bearing several tons of massive muscles, a growing elephant could easily snap a small chain or pull a small peg out of the ground. So, do the circus workers have to attach bigger and bigger chains to the shackle on the elephant's leg? No. The elephant has been conditioned. The small chain and small peg seems to a permanent prison in the elephant's mind. In fact, the mind of the elephant is imprisoned more than its body. What it believes severely limits the actions of its body.

The same is true of you: what you believe controls the possibilities open to you in life. If you believe you are controlled by fate or poverty or what people say about you, you'll never thrive as God intended. But suppose the grown elephant realized its God-given strength and broke free from its flimsy bonds and escaped to the freedom of the forest. It could begin to flourish in the full and free life that God intends. And what if your eyes were opened to the flimsy mental chains that limit your potential? What if you got a true glimpse of who you are and why you're here? Then you could begin living into your true identity and purpose that God has revealed in His Word. That's what this course is all about. Do you want that?

[Give out laminated "Course One Overview" from appendix to each student. Go over the structure of the course, explaining the curriculum's overall title (Opportunity Makers), subtitle (24 Seeds for a Fruitful Future), front cover image (mango tree painting on front cover) and purpose ("nurture the mindset, relationships and habits that can grow a fruitful future in your life and community").]

I want to share with you a key passage of Scripture which clearly shows the kind of person this course aims to help you become: an "opportunity maker" who is nurturing seeds that will grow into a "fruitful future" for your entire community. Please listen closely to 2 Corinthians 9:6-11: "Remember this: The person who plants a little will have a small harvest. But the person who plants a lot will have a big harvest. Each one should give, then, what he has decided in his heart to give. He should not give if it makes him sad. And he should not give if he thinks he is forced to give. God loves the person who gives happily. And God can give you more blessings than you need. Then you will always have plenty of everything. You will have enough to give to every good work.

It is written in the Scriptures: "He gives freely to the poor. The things he does are right and will continue forever." God is the One who gives seed to the farmer. And he gives bread for food. And God will give you all the seed you need and make it grow. He will make a great harvest from your goodness. God will make you rich in every way so that you can always give freely. And your giving through us will cause many to give thanks to God."

In this passage, God boldly promises to keep heaping blessings upon you when you keep sharing them with others. This passage pictures you as the happiest person in the world. As you give to others, God gives you even more. Not only are you satisfied with a big harvest of fruit in your own life, so are your neighbors. And best of all, you become a co-worker with God in producing that harvest. Wow! Don't you want that? Your abundant generosity even helps people grow closer to God as it evokes prayers of thanksgiving.

A. Introducing Opportunity Makers

[Give the following overview of each course:]

Course One: This is the course we're starting today.

- Title: "12 Truths to Nourish Your Soul."
- Identity and Purpose Statements. This entire course is built on these two statements. Please listen closely:
  - "WHO I AM: **I am a cherished child of God with immense value and important responsibility. God gives me joy in healthy relationships with Him, His earth, and other people. God is working to restore me and my relationships to reflect Him beautifully.**"
  - "WHY I'M HERE: **God's good plan for me is to nurture the seeds He gives into strong talents to serve Him by serving others. I can be very generous with others because I can trust God to take care of me. He helps my talents bear much fruit that blesses people and God's earth. This pleases the Lord, shows His love to people, and brings me joy. This good work is practice for reigning with Jesus in His Kingdom.**"

  These statements are drawn from God's Word which holds immense power to transform us. It plants seeds in our souls that bear good fruit to bless many.
- 12 Truths and 12 Lies [Read to the class the first sentence of each truth and each lie from 12 Truths and 12 Lies in the Appendix.] Note that #1-5 relate to identity – who I am – and #6-12 relate to purpose – why I'm here. The lies are like the small peg that imprison the powerful elephant. When we realize that we can break free from them, we can live into the liberating truths of our biblical identity and purpose.
- Joseph. To make it real, we'll explore the life of Joseph from the Bible. We think you'll be amazed at how beautifully Joseph's life illustrates all 12 truths. He is an excellent example for you to follow. Teaching 12 truths through a flesh-and-blood life will make them real for you. It will show you – not just tell you – how these 12 truths can be lived out in life's trials.

Course Two: This is the next course after this one. [Share this section only if your organization plans to offer Course Two soon after Course One.]

- Course Two is meant to help you integrate your biblical identity and purpose into your real life. It's good to know who you are and why you are here, but unless you let these powerful seeds sprout you're your mind into your actions, they cannot produce a fruitful future. There's a big difference between knowing something is true and being transformed as it shapes your life. Knowing what a bicycle looks like is vastly inferior to feeling the breeze in your hair as you peddle through a beautiful day! Recent research shows that you've not completely learned something until you practice it. You have to get on and ride. We already knew this from Bible verses like "faith without work is dead" (James 2:17) and "blessed are those who hear and put into practice these words of mine" (Luke 11:28). For those of you who are serious about living out the 12 truths you'll learn in this course, we have a second Opportunity Makers course which you can take. It is called "12 Habits to Co-Create with God". Like I said, it will help you to integrate your biblical identity and purpose into your daily life.

But I must warn you: the commitment is much higher than in course one. It will be more about what you do in between classes than what happens during class. In fact, it will ask you to change how you spend your time every day. That's asking a lot because change is really hard. But because the changes are based on God's Word, they will be very good for you and your future. Now that you've learned what a bicycle is and what it does, it's time to hop on and learn to ride it. Yes, it is scary and dangerous, but moving through life in a whole new way will bring you freedom and joy!

- Why is Course Two built upon habits? Because forming new habits is a powerful way to change your life. Let's read the 12 habits that Course Two will show you how to build into your life. [Read the 12 habits from page 4 of the Opportunity Makers Overview in the Appendix.]
- Course Two is not for everyone because it requires a high commitment every day as it asks you to change your daily habits. It is only for those who are really serious about changing their lives. In fact, both Course One and Course Two have potential to powerfully shape the rest of your life for good – leading to a fruitful future. But *only* if you have a strong desire to be transformed by the truths of God's Word. *Only* if you focus on learning all you can during the course. *Only* if you open your heart and warmly embrace the truth of who you are and why you're here. *Only* if you do your homework and stay connected with your accountability partner. [Explain what you want them to do with their partner in between each lesson.]

Actually, you'll a few minutes right now with your accountability partner.

[Break into pairs and have them answer these two questions, then pray for each other]

What do you hope to gain from this course?

Where and when will we get together in between lessons?

Closing Prayer. [Bring class together for a final prayer for God to bless them abundantly through Opportunity Makers.]

B. Introducing Identity and Purpose

Requirements.
- **Time.** [The lessons contain roughly 60 minutes of material.]
- **Supplies.** [See Introduction for general supplies needed for every lesson.]

Opening Prayer. [Pray.]

[Have a few students share for each of the following questions.]

Tell me something that is true.

Tell me something that is false.

What is truth? [Discuss.]

    [Hint:]

- A truth is a statement that matches reality. It is the opposite of a lie which denies or distorts the truth.

Why is truth important? [Discuss.]

    [Hint:]

- What we think is true has a big influence on how we live. Being out of touch with reality is harmful and sometimes dangerous.

How can getting our identity and purpose wrong be disastrous? [Discuss.]

If someone sends you down the wrong road to the soccer stadium, you might miss the game. But if you get bad directions to the hospital in an emergency, not knowing the truth could be far more serious.

And two of the most important truths to know are "who you are" and "why you're here". "Who you are" refers to your identity – how you see yourself as a person. "Why you're here" refers to your purpose – what role you are created to fulfill. Both identity and purpose speak to our value – to God, people, and ourselves. Whether you see yourself as worthless or extremely valuable makes a huge difference in your life. Let's break into groups of six and imagine how these beliefs can shape a life.

How would a young person's life turn out when believing this statement about oneself:

    Debora beliefs that "I am extremely valuable to God and he has given me an important job to do."

[Give the previous statement to half of the groups and the following statement to the other half of them.]

    Oscar believes that "I am worthless, and my life has no meaning."

Create a story with as much details as possible. Choose one person to take notes and share your story with the whole class.

[Give groups 3-4 minutes to discuss, then regather the class to hear their stories.]

Notice how different Debora and Oscar's lives are. Why are beliefs about identity and purpose so powerful? [Discuss.] Lies about "who you are" and "why you're here" don't just misinform you, they distort you. They poison your heart and mind. This throws you off the course God intended for your life.

On the other hand, embracing God's truth about your identity and purpose can heal your soul and transform your life – for the rest of your days. That's what this Opportunity Makers course is all about. Course One is named "12 Truths To Nourish Your Soul" and we'll take whole lessons to explore each of the 12 truths – 5 about 'identity' and 7 about 'purpose'. Do you want to take a quick preview of what you'll be learning about in the next 12 lessons?

[Display the identity and purpose statements on the whiteboard along with the lesson titles.]

The next 5 lessons will be based on this identity statement:

> "WHO I AM: **I am a cherished child of God with immense value and important responsibility. God gives me joy in healthy relationships with Him, His earth, and other people. God is working to restore me and my relationships to reflect Him beautifully.**"

[Have a student with a bold and cheerful voice repeat it.]

What do you learn about yourself from this statement? [Discuss.]

There are five truths from this statement that we'll study closely – one per lesson. Here's a quick look at the five lessons based on this overall statement of biblical identity we just read…

[Read truths 1-5 from 12 Truths At-a-Glance in the Appendix.]

The last 7 of these 12 truths to nourish your soul are about God's purpose for you. These seven lessons are based on this statement of biblical purpose:

> "WHY I'M HERE: **God's good plan for me is to nurture the seeds He gives into strong talents to serve Him by serving others. I can be very generous with others because I can trust God to take care of me. He helps my talents bear much fruit that blesses people and God's earth. This pleases the Lord, shows His love to people, and brings me joy. This good work is practice for reigning with Jesus in His Kingdom.**"

[Have a student with a bold and cheerful voice repeat it.]

There are seven truths from this statement that we'll study closely – one per lesson. Let's take a quick look at the seven lessons based on the overall statement of biblical purpose we just read…

[Read truths 6-12 from 12 Truths At-a-Glance in the Appendix.]

B. Introducing Identity and Purpose

Which of these truths will nourish your soul the most?

[Read them again pausing after each to have them raise their hand to indicate the one they think will bless them the most.]

Suppose you received a bicycle as a gift but you had to put it together yourself, would you rather use this diagram on these directions to assemble it? [Show the two images from the appendix and discuss.]

Why do most people find it easier to follow a picture? [Discuss.]

The Bible doesn't just *tell* us these truths; it *shows* them to use in real, flesh and blood lives. The Bible is full of stories of people who lived these truths well – and many who did not. To help you see how embracing these 12 truths can shape you, we'll look at how Joseph embodied each of these truths in his life. Our next lesson will take a close look at Joseph's life to give you an example to follow, then we'll look at parts of his story in each of the 12 truth lessons. You'll also see how these truths shine perfectly in the life of our Lord Jesus who calls us to follow Him. Although Jesus is fully God, He is also fully human so He experienced trials and limitations just like you. So, Jesus and Joseph will bring these truths to life for you, giving you footprints to follow.

In fact, here is a quick look at the identity and purpose of Jesus. Let's listen to John 13:1-5:

> "It was almost time for the Jewish Passover Feast. Jesus knew that it was time for him to leave this world and go back to the Father. He had always loved those who were his own in the world, and he loved them all the way to the end. Jesus and his followers were at the evening meal. The devil had already persuaded Judas Iscariot to turn against Jesus. (Judas was the son of Simon.) Jesus knew that the Father had given him power over everything. He also knew that he had come from God and was going back to God. So during the meal Jesus stood up and took off his outer clothing. Taking a towel, he wrapped it around his waist. Then he poured water into a bowl and began to wash the followers' feet. He dried them with the towel that was wrapped around him."

What was Jesus' understanding of His own identity and purpose? [Discuss.]

What did that knowledge about Himself lead Him to do? [Discuss.]

How does this apply to our own lives? [Discuss.]

   [Hint:]
   - A firm grasp on the truth of who we are gives us the confidence to do difficult things that will benefit others.

What would happen in your own life if you thoroughly believed the biblical truths of your identity and purpose? [Discuss.]

Closing Prayer: [Pray for these 12 truths to transform students' lives.]

C. Introducing the Life of Joseph

Requirements.
- **Time.** The lessons contain roughly 60 minutes of material.
- **Supplies.** Colored markers and paper plus tape to attach paper to the wall.

Opening Prayer. [Pray.]

As we said in the previous lesson, Joseph will be your primary example of how to live out the 12 truths about "who you are" and "why you're here", so this lesson will take you deep into his life story.

Who is familiar with the story of Joseph in Genesis, the first book of the Bible? [Raise hands.]

He was one of the 12 sons of Jacob who was also called Israel. Joseph was also a great-grandson of Abraham, the great father of faith. What do you remember about Joseph's story? [Discuss.]

The story is told in 13 chapters at the end of Genesis, but twice in later parts of the Bible his story is summarized in only seven short verses. Let's listen to both passages.

Please listen to Psalm 105:16-22:

> "God ordered a time of hunger in the land. And he destroyed all the food.
>
> Then he sent a man ahead of them. It was Joseph, who was sold as a slave.
>
> They put chains around his feet and an iron ring around his neck.
>
> Then the time he had spoken of came. The Lord's words proved that Joseph was right.
>
> The king of Egypt sent for Joseph and freed him. The ruler of the people set him free.
>
> He made him the master of his house. Joseph was in charge of his riches.
>
> He could order the princes as he wished. He taught the older men to be wise."

Now please listen to Acts 7:9-14:

> "These sons became jealous of Joseph. They sold him to be a slave in Egypt. But God was with him. Joseph had many troubles there, but God saved him from all those troubles. The king of Egypt liked Joseph and respected him because of the wisdom that God gave him. The king made him governor of Egypt. He put Joseph in charge of all the people in his palace. "Then all the land of Egypt and of Canaan became so dry that nothing would grow there. This made the people suffer very much. The sons could not find anything to eat. But when Jacob heard that there was grain in Egypt, he sent his sons, our ancestors, there. This was their first trip to

Egypt. Then they went there a second time. This time, Joseph told his brothers who he was. And the king learned about Joseph's family. Then Joseph sent some men to invite Jacob, his father, to come to Egypt. He also invited all his relatives - 75 persons altogether."

Those quick overviews are like fast-forwarding through a movie or seeing a new place only from high above in an airplane. You get a true picture, but you can't see the small details. So, let's go a little deeper by looking at the longer story in Genesis. We'll break it up into seven scenes. [Break class into seven groups and assign each of the following scenes from Joseph's life for them to read. Before class, write the Scripture references on seven pieces of paper so you don't have to take time to repeat them verbally. [Pass out paper and markers.]

Genesis 37:1-36	Genesis 39:1-20	Genesis 49:1-33; 50:15-21
Genesis 39:20-40:23	Genesis 41:1-32	
Genesis 41:33-57	Genesis 42:1-10; 45:1-15	

Read the passage out loud as a group, then decide how you will act out the scene for the rest of the class. This will be a mime, so choose a narrator to explain what the silent actors are doing. Only the narrator will speak while the others act out the scene. Also, choose a title for your scene and have one person write the title in large, fancy letters on the paper I gave each group.

[Give students 10 minutes to read and prepare their mimes and signs. Have adults walk around to keep the groups moving quickly to prepare each part of their assignments. Then give each group two minutes to present their mime with narration, taping their signs with the names of the scenes on the wall in order.]

Good job acting out the life of Joseph! Now to tie these scenes all together, let's look at a timeline that shares the major events in Joseph's life.

[Pass out copies of "Timeline of Joseph's Life" from the appendix and write it out on the whiteboard if possible. Have two volunteers read alternating lines until they've read through the entire timeline.]

Let's discuss the life of Joseph: Raise your hands to answer the following questions.
- What in this story surprised you?
- Who faced more trials in life – you or Joseph?
- Who experienced more trust in God – you or Joseph? Raise hands to answer.
- How did Joseph continue to keep a positive attitude during 13 years of suffering?
- What did Joseph believe about God?
- What did Joseph believe about himself?

C. Introducing the Life of Joseph

- What did Joseph believe about his future?
- What did Joseph do every day that helped shape a fruitful future?

[If time allows and the media is available in your language, play or display the story of Joseph. Possibilities include audio or video recordings of Genesis 37, 39-50, The Bible Project video from YouTube, or a cartoon book that tells the story of Joseph.]

Closing Prayer. Let's break into trios and pray for each other to have strength to follow Joseph's example of trust in God even during trials.

[Bring class back together and lead them in a closing prayer, asking God to grow in your students' traits that Joseph embodied.]

1. Who I Am: Defined by God

Supplies – You will need one good mirror and one cracked mirror. If a cracked mirror is not available, you can use a photograph of someone's reflection in a cracked or distorted (carnival) mirror (plus standard supplies listed in the Introduction).

FIRST HALF – 45 minutes

Review Previous Lesson's Homework. [Have each adult lead a small group of students in sharing how their homework went. Adults record who did their homework as credit toward graduation.]

Share the title of today's lesson and how it fits into the course as a whole. [Review with students the "Opportunity Makers Overview" from the Appendix to remind them of how today's lesson connects to what they have been learning. For example remind them of the Identity Statement (for lessons 1-5) or Purpose Statement (for lessons 6-12) and the truths from previous lessons. If possible, show these things on the whiteboard as well.]

Opening Prayer. [Pray]

Student Activity.

- **Explain.** [Write these 3 messages on separate slips of paper one message per slip:

  "I am better than you."   "You are better than me."   "We are each dearly cherished by God."

  Prepare enough slips for each student in the class to have three. Recruit three student volunteers. The first volunteer passes out an "I am better than you are" slip to each student.]

- **Do.** [Read the message out loud to the class.] Think about this message silently.

  [After 15 seconds of silence, have the second volunteer pass out the "you are better than me" slip to each student. Read the message out loud to the class.] Think about this message silently.

  [After 15 seconds of silence, have the third volunteer pass out the "we are each dearly cherished by God" slip to each student. Read the message out loud to the class.] Think about this message silently.

- **Debrief.** [After 15 seconds of silence, ask students the following questions and affirm their replies…]
  a. How did you feel after reading "I am better than you"?

b. How did you feel after reading "you are better than me"?

c. How did you feel after reading "we are each dearly cherish by God"?

d. "Which of these three messages are true?"

e. "What happens when we believe the first or second message?"

[Listen to and affirm the responses of the students.]

Believing those lies gives us a distorted picture of ourselves – either above or below other people. But who we are is not a comparison with other people but an identity given to us by God. We are defined by God's immeasurable love.

[Show students their reflection in a mirror that is cracked and then in a mirror that is whole. If a cracked mirror is not available, show students a photograph of someone's reflection in a broken or distorted carnival mirror.]

Have you been looking at your soul in a broken or a whole mirror?

Teach the Truth and Lie.

- **Transition.** Here is what the true mirror of God's Word tells you about yourself…

- **Read the Truth and Lie.** Today's entire lesson is built upon this biblical truth. Please read it aloud with me [from whiteboard or poster on wall where students can be reminded of the topic throughout the lesson].

    > **Truth about my identity: I am defined by God's love, not my own thoughts, nor by the actions or words of people.** While parents and peers try to shape my self-image, only my Heavenly Father's perspective ultimately matters. When God looks at me, he sees the righteousness of Jesus in whom I trust.

    > **Lie about my identity: I am defined by my family, home, and possessions.** I am lower than others, so I deserve whatever evil is said or done to me. I am unloved and unlovable.

- **Explain.** God's love can cast out fear of what others think of you. God's Word can drown out any lie spoken about you. God's power can shield your soul from any attack. [Explain the truth further in your own words if necessary.]

- **Support with Scripture.** Knowing who you truly are is a solid foundation to build your life upon. When God's authority, power, presence, and love is on your side, you can laugh at things that used to devastate you. Listen to Romans 8:31: "So, what should we say about this? If God is for us, then no one can defeat us."

- **Illustrate.** What is your favorite thing that you ever made?

1. Who I Am: Defined by God

It could be a drawing, painting, bracelet, poem, song, story, trail, fort, treehouse, garden, toy, game, piece of clothing, and something out of wood. [Display this list if possible.]

Think for a minute and pick one. Now share in trios what it was and what you liked about it."

[Give them two minutes to discuss it, then regather in whole group. Have them share a few examples with the whole class. Optional: share about something you yourself made as a child and show it your students if possible.]

How much did you love what you made? 1= ok, 2 = good, 3 = made me smile, 4 = thoroughly enjoyed it, 5 = awesome, amazing, I delight in it!

"Would you have liked it just as much if someone else had made it? Why or why not? [Discuss why.]

God likes what He made too! No – He *loves* what He creates. You like a lot of things you've made, but today you shared your favorite.

Well, the Bible shows us that *we* are God's favorite creation! He saved the best for last. Humans were His final creation and He took extra time to carefully form them, then He breathed into them the breath of life. We are the only creatures He created in His own image, His own likeness. We'll learn more about this in a future lesson, but we can do God-like things that animals cannot and we mere creatures have been given responsibility over the rest of creation. Unbelievable! So says Psalm 8:4-8:

> "But why is man important to you? Why do you take care of human beings? You made man a little lower than the angels. And you crowned him with glory and honor. You put him in charge of everything you made. You put all things under his control: all the sheep, the cattle and the wild animals, the birds in the sky, the fish in the sea, and everything that lives under water."

That's a lot of trust God puts in us! In addition to the Bible, what other evidence do you have that God lovingly created you and delights in you?

[Hints.]

- Intricacy of your body and it's many abilities.
- Capacity of your heart to love.
- Capacity of your mind to think, reason, communicate and create.
- You are absolutely unique – one of a kind. Of all the billions of people, there has never been someone like you and never will be!

[Discuss.]

What are some of the most valuable things people can buy? (Cars, houses, artwork, jewels, land.)? Often, the fewer number of items like it, the more expensive something is. Did you notice this fact? The most expensive things are one of a kind – pieces of art. The Bible says: We are God's masterpiece. [Ephesians 2:10]

Example of Joseph.

- **Transition.** Knowing you are one of God's masterpieces gives you a strong leg to stand on in life. Knowing that other people are equally valuable to God keeps the first truth in balance. It is the other leg. Not valuing others dishonors your Creator's opinion of them. When you stop listening to God, you start taking His credit for the gifts He's given you. Putting yourself above others is like having one long leg and one short leg: neither one will work right!

- **Read from Genesis.** [Read Genesis 37:1-4.]

- **Discuss.** Jacob was wrong to show more love to Joseph than to his other 11 sons. This caused Joseph and his brothers to believe lies about themselves and compare themselves with each other. The special treatment that Joseph received distorted their views of themselves and their relationships with each other. What was in their hearts soon came out in their actions.

Closing Prayer. [Thank God for key biblical insights uncovered during the lesson.]

1. Who I Am: Defined by God

SECOND HALF – 45 minutes

Opening Prayer. [Pray]

Re-read Truth and Lie.

> ➢ **Truth about my identity: I am defined by God's love, not my own thoughts, nor by the actions or words of people.** While parents and peers try to shape my self-image, only my Heavenly Father's perspective ultimately matters. When God looks at me, he sees the righteousness of Jesus in whom I trust.
>
> ➢ **Lie about my identity: I am defined by my family, home, and possessions.** I am lower than others, so I deserve whatever evil is said or done to me. I am unloved and unlovable.

Imagination Exercise.

- **Directions.** "What are several things that happened to Joseph that told him he was no good?"
  [On a whiteboard or flipchart, list what the students say in order of when they happened to Joseph. Then fill in the events the students missed and review the completed list. You may want to draw a downward spiral next to the list and describe the progression as such. Your list may look something like this: DOWNWARD SPIRAL OF HOW MUCH PEOPLE VALUED JOSEPH: Favorite son > hated by brothers > physically abused > betrayed and sold by brothers > separated from his father > taken from his homeland > enslaved > falsely accused > imprisoned > forgotten. Ask the class to close their eyes and pretend they are Joseph while you read the list to them again.]

- **Discuss.** [Ask them to write down their answers to the following.]
  How will you hold onto God's view of yourself when your daily experience says you are worthless?
  [Give them a minute or two to write down their thoughts, then discuss their ideas with them.]
  Which of these ideas can you use when inner thoughts or outer circumstances say you are unloved?

Summary.

- **Summary Statement.** Nothing and no one but God can define you. Only He has the right to tell you who you are. And only He is correct. God loves what He creates, and you are the pinnacle of His Creation. When others try to push you down or when you try to push others down, your view of yourself can be distorted like a cracked mirror. Only the true mirror of God's Word, especially the life and death of Jesus, can show you the value that God's immeasurable love gives you.

- **Example of Jesus.** Would you rather have a letter from a loving parent or both a letter and a hug? The Old Testament is a letter to you that gives many examples of a Heavenly Father lovingly pursuing His rebellious children. But Jesus shines light on God's love in a whole new way, on a whole new level. He brought the Father's hug. Reading about God's love is beautiful, but Jesus brought it here in flesh and blood! And way more than a hug, Jesus took our worst and gave us God's best. Here's how the Apostle Paul puts it in 2 Corinthians 8:9:

    > "You know the grace of our Lord Jesus Christ. You know that Christ was rich, but for you he became poor. Christ did this so that by his being poor you might become rich."

    Jesus took our sin, shame, and death. As He walked the earth, the way He cared for every part of people's lives shows us God's love: He fed the hungry bodies, He taught ignorant minds, He freed people from sickness, and evil spirits. He did not heal crowd from a stage. No, he touched individual people, looked them in the eyes, and spoke tenderly to them. For example, here is what Jesus did when a 12-year-old girl died in Mark 5:40-42:

    > "But they only laughed at Jesus. He told all the people to leave. Then he went into the room where the child was. He took the child's father and mother and his three followers into the room with him. 41 Then he took hold of the girl's hand and said to her, "Talitha, koum!" (This means, "Little girl, I tell you to stand up!") 42 The girl stood right up and began walking. (She was 12 years old.) The father and mother and the followers were amazed."

    Instead of bringing her dead body outside where a huge crowd could see a spectacular miracle, He gave her and her family privacy, took her by the hand and spoke to her so that she lived. The voice of Jesus also gives us life. He speaks the Father's love and forgiveness into our souls, lets us know we are worth dying for, provides for our daily needs, and promises to raise our bodies to new life in the end.

- **Summary Scripture.** Listen to Psalm 27:10-14:

    > "If my father and mother leave me, the Lord will take me in. Lord, teach me your ways. Guide me to do what is right because I have enemies. Do not let my enemies defeat me. They tell lies about me. They say they will hurt me. I truly believe I will live to see the Lord's goodness. Wait for the Lord's help. Be strong and brave and wait for the Lord's help."

    People do hurt us by their words and actions, but there is a limit to the damage they can do because we know deep down that God's love for us has the final word!

- **Summary Questions.** [Instruct students to give a thumbs up/down sign or shout out yes/no.]
    (1) Is God the only one who can tell you who you are? *Yes*

1. Who I Am: Defined by God

(2) Does it really matter what other people say or do to you? *No*

(3) Does your value in God's eyes depend on where you live or what your family owns? *No*

(4) Are you higher than other people? *No*

(5) Are you lower than other people? *No*

(6) Does the abundant love of God say you're worth more than a mountain of gold? *Yes*

(7) Can knowing who God says you are shield you from lies you are tempted to believe? *Yes*

(8) Does Jesus' tender care for people show you how God feels about you? *Yes*

Assign Homework.

- **Option A.** Find someone you've mistreated. Apologize and tell them how much God loves them.
- **Option B.** Thank God for his great love. Write one of today's scriptures (Romans 8:31, Genesis 37:1-4, 2 Corinthians 8:9, and Psalm 27:10-14) on a piece of paper and read it every day this week. Ask God to show you more of his love.

Closing Prayer. [If time is short, pray for the students. Otherwise, ask students to pray in pairs or small groups.]

2. Who I Am: Cherished Child

FIRST HALF – 45 minutes

Review Previous Lesson's Homework. [Have each adult lead a small group of students in sharing how their homework went. Adults record who did their homework as credit toward graduation.]

Share the title of today's lesson and how it fits into the course as a whole. [Review with students the "Opportunity Makers Overview" from the Appendix to remind them of how today's lesson connects to what they have been learning. For example remind them of the Identity Statement (for lessons 1-5) or Purpose Statement (for lessons 6-12) and the truths from previous lessons. If possible, show these things on the whiteboard as well.]

Opening Prayer.

Student Activity.

- **Explain.** [Give each child a hug while reading identity truth #2 to him/her, changing "me" and "I" to "you". If the class is large, your adult assistants can join you in this. If giving hugs is awkward, say this instead… "Think of a time you felt greatly loved by a parent or grandparent when receiving from them a gift, a hug, a kind word, a special meal or outing."]

- **Do.** [Give out hugs or give students time to reflect on the question about feeling loved.]

- **Debrief.** [Ask the following questions one at a time and discuss with the class…]
    a. "How did this experience make you feel?"
    b. If an imperfect person can show such love, what does this teach you about the kind of love that the perfect God has for you?
    c. What did it cost your teacher, parent, or grandparent to show love to you?
    d. What did it cost God to show you even greater love?
    [Hint:]
    - He sent his only Son to die for you!

Teach the Truth and Lie.

- **Transition.** "Even the best human love is only a faint echo of God's roaring love for you!"

- **Read the Truth and Lie.** Today's entire lesson is built upon this biblical truth. Please read it aloud with me [from whiteboard or poster on wall where students can be reminded of the topic throughout the lesson].
    - ➢ **Truth about my identity: God lovingly created me and delights in me.** I have immeasurable value because God created me in His image and made me one of His royal representatives. I am a cherished child of a loving Heavenly Father who allowed His Son to die to restore me to Himself.
    - ➢ **Lie about my identity: If God even exists, he has forgotten me.** I am of little value to anyone. I am worthless. I am no good. I am poor. I am a burden.

- **Explain.** [Explain the truth further in your own words if necessary.] God's opinion of you is what really matters and here's a Bible verse that proves how much he values you….

- **Support with Scripture.** Read Listen to Romans 8:32: "If God already gave us what was most precious to him – his Son – he will keep showing us his amazing love forever!" "God has already paid the highest price to restore a right relationship to you. The love of the cross is our guarantee of His undying love – today, tomorrow and throughout eternity!"

- **Illustrate.** Who do you let tell you who you are and what you're worth? Many voices try to set your identity and value. Which voice do you listen to? Whose ideas about yourself do you embrace deep in your heart? Many of us grow up with voices saying we're worthless. It might be a parent, classmates, or even your own inner voice. When these negative voices echo in your ears all day, every day, it's almost impossible to deny them. They become ingrained. But here's good news: it doesn't mean they're true! There are commonly accepted ideas in everyday life that are not true either. For example, we say "the sun rises" and "the sun sets." We can watch it move across our sky with our own eyes. How is that for undeniable evidence? But we know from science that the sun is not moving around the earth. In fact, the opposite is true. The earth is spinning so that it seems that the sun rises and sets. The same is true of the negative voices that try to define you. Just because you and others have believed them doesn't make them true. In fact, the exact opposite is true. You are defined by God's love, not by your own thoughts, nor by the actions or words of others.

Example of Joseph.

- **Transition.** "How can we hold onto this truth when people don't love us like God does? When they hurt us rather than hug us? Let's look at the example of godly young Joseph for guidance.

- **Read from Genesis.** Read Genesis 37:18-28 out loud to the class, asking them to imagine that they are Joseph in the story.

- **Discuss.** What do you think Joseph was feeling and thinking during this difficult part of his life? [Discuss] Even though his brothers didn't love him, Joseph knew that he was valuable because God loved him. When his brothers threw him in a pit, then sold him as a slave to people from another country, he did not give up. Instead, he believed that God was with him even though life was hard. Then things got even worse! Were you ever accused of doing something wrong that you did not do? [Raise hands.] That happened to Joseph when he was working very hard as a slave. When he was accused of doing wrong, he was sent to jail. Even in jail, he still believed that God loved him very much and had an important job for him to do.

    The same is true for you. Even when bad things happen to you, you can trust in God's love. He loves you *so* much that He allowed His Son to die so that you can become one of His precious sons and daughters! Nothing anyone can say or do to you can destroy the value that God has woven into you. God put more of Himself into us than anything else He created! Since God put His own goodness in us, nothing bad that we do or is done to us can ever erase it. God deposited permanent value into each person He carefully crafted. Amen?

Closing Prayer. [Thank God for key biblical insights uncovered during the lesson.]

SECOND HALF – 45 minutes

Opening Prayer. [Pray.]

Re-read Truth and Lie.

> - **Truth about my identity: God lovingly created me and delights in me.** I have immeasurable value because God created me in His image and made me one of His royal representatives. I am a cherished child of a loving Heavenly Father who allowed His Son to die to restore me to Himself.
> - **Lie about my identity: If God even exists, he has forgotten me.** I am of little value to anyone. I am worthless. I am no good. I am poor. I am a burden.

Imagination Exercise.

- **Read from Genesis.** [Read Genesis 37:26-28.]

- **Directions.** "Close eyes and imagine that you have also just been sold into slavery along with Joseph. Imagine that you are on the camel with Joseph being taken to Egypt and you are feeling worthless and forgotten by God. What do you think the 17-year-old Joseph would say to encourage you? Take a couple of minutes of silence to think and write about this question before we discuss it."

  [Have a few students share their answers with the whole class.]

- **Discuss.** "Please close your eyes and listen to what I think Joseph might say to you on the camel ride into slavery: 'Think about the stories your parents or grandparents read to you. Remember that often hard things happen in the middle of the story, but everything turns out right in the end. God is writing our story right now. He's with us during the hard times and is using them to grow our strength and patience. He will use us in His story to help others and He will make sure the end of the story turns out well for us too!'

  Joseph might also say: 'Think of a time you felt very close to God…Go ahead and take a moment to remember…. Even though we are being taken away from our families and being sold as slaves, God is with us right now, shares our pain, and loves us very, very much! To God, you are *not* a slave but a royal son or daughter with an important job to do for Him. God doesn't think you are worthless, and *His* opinion is what counts! He will even use us to show himself to others. So, don't let wrong things people do to you make you feel worthless. Even though it doesn't seem like it, God is still in control and will bring good out of this evil."

  [Switching from Joseph's voice to your own, ask the following question….]
  As you rode on the camel with Joseph, how did his words make you feel?

2. Who I Am: Cherished Child

Summary.

- **Summary Statement.** Bad things that happen to you cannot steal your good identity. What others think, say or do cannot change the most important truth about you: God is wildly in love with you! As His cherished child, your value is beyond measure. This is confirmed by the facts that God has made you in His image, given you the important role of representing Him, and allowed His only Son to die to give you new life. These truths can give you confidence that God's delight in you has only just begun!

- **Example of Jesus.** When Jesus walked the roads of Palestine 2000 years ago, the most shameful thing to be was a leper. Not only did they have a terrible skin disease, but they were also treated like dirty people. In fact, they had to live with other lepers in a separate place away from other people. But Jesus didn't accept this negative judgment on lepers. Listen to what happened when he met a leper in Mark 1:40-42:

    "A man who had a harmful skin disease came to Jesus. The man fell to his knees and begged Jesus, 'I know that you can heal me if you will.' Jesus felt sorry for the man. So, he touched him and said, 'I want to heal you. Be healed!' At once the disease left the man, and he was healed.'"

    Instead of believing the other voices about lepers, Jesus was moved with compassion. Instead of staying far away, He even touched him and valued him enough to heal him of his painful disease. Jesus knows that what is wrong with you does not define you. God's grace and mercy defines you.

- **Summary Scripture.** Listen to Psalm 139:13-14: "You made my whole being. You formed me in my mother's body. I praise you because you made me in an amazing and wonderful way. What you have done is wonderful. I know this very well." Each of you were lovingly put together by God Himself in your mother's womb. God thought about what special gifts and personality traits to give you. He made you into a one-of-a-kind masterpiece. There's no one like you, so you can glorify God in a unique way.

    Summary Questions. [Instruct students to give a thumbs up/down sign or shout out yes/no.]

    (1) Did Joseph's troubles mean that God had forgotten him? *No*

    (2) When people mistreat you, does it mean you are worthless? *No*

    (3) Is God with you always and does he share your pain? *Yes*

    (4) Will God use troubles to shape you? *Yes*

    (5) Will God work out all things for your good in the end? *Yes*

    (6) Can you trust God with the story of your life? *Yes*

    (7) Does God love you enough to allow his Son to die for you? *Yes*

(8) Does God have an important job for you to do for him? *Yes*

Assign Homework.

- **Option A.** Ask someone going through a hard time to tell you how they are feeling. Remind them that God loves them, is with them, and feels their pain. Give them a smile or a hug and pray for them.

- **Option B.** Think about a problem you have. Give it to God and ask him to show you that he is near. Tell him you trust him to take care of you. Pray that God will give you strength and use this problem to help you grow.

Closing Prayer. [If time is short, pray for the students. Otherwise, ask students to pray in pairs or small groups.] "Let's pray through a Scripture passage that powerfully reinforces what we've learned today. I'm going to read Romans 8:14-18 as our prayer, and every time I say 'we' or 'us', I want you to boldly say the name of our group [such as 'Church of God students']. Ready?

"Dear Father, as your cherished children, WE claim these amazing promises from your Word: 'The true children of God are those who let God's Spirit lead them. The Spirit that WE received is not a spirit that makes US slaves again to fear. The Spirit that WE have makes US children of God. And with that Spirit WE say, "Father, dear Father." And the Spirit himself joins with our spirits to say that WE are God's children. If WE are God's children, then WE will receive the blessings God has for US. WE will receive these things from God together with Christ. But WE must suffer as Christ suffered, and then WE will have glory as Christ has glory. WE have sufferings now. But the sufferings WE have now are nothing compared to the great glory that will be given to US."

- A healthy tree may give you shade, fruit, oxygen, beauty, wood, medicine, enriched soil, and homes for birds and other wildlife.

So, you can see that healthy relationships multiply good for everyone!

Example of Joseph.

- **Transition.** Joseph was 17 years old when his brother sold him as a slave and for 13 years, he had more difficulties until finally God promoted him from the prison to the throne. In both the hardships and the triumph, God was with him every step of the way. Then in his ninth year of working for the King, God made it possible for Joseph and his brothers to be reunited. What do you think happened when they saw each other for the first time in 22 years? [Discuss.] Was Joseph angry all those years? Did he hold a grudge and plot how he would take revenge against them if he ever saw them again? [Discuss.]

- **Read from Genesis.** [Read Genesis 45:1-8, 14-15.]

- **Discuss.** Why didn't Joseph use his power to punish or kill them? Here is his secret to not repay their evil with evil…. [Read Genesis 50:17-21.] He knew that God was still in control and would bring something good out of the evil that his brothers had done to him. This is a great example of how trusting God helps us to have healthy relationships with our fellow sinners.

Closing Prayer. [Thank God for key biblical insights uncovered during the lesson.]

SECOND HALF – 45 minutes

Opening Prayer. [Pray.]

Re-read Truth and Lie.

> - **Truth about my identity: I was created for intimacy, to enjoy harmony with God, people and God's earth.** While our sin has damaged all of these relationships, God is working to heal them.
> - **Lie about my identity: I don't need anyone else.** I must look out for myself because people will only harm me. The strong always trample the weak.

Imagination Exercise.

- **Directions.** Imagine that you are one of Joseph's 11 brothers. If you're a boy, choose a name from this list: Reuben, Simeon, Levi, Judah, Dan, Naphtali, Gad, Asher, Issachar, Zebulun, and Benjamin. If you're a girl, change one of these names to a girl's name. Close your eyes and imagine you are having dinner when Joseph tells you who he really is. Knowing that you had helped to sell him as a slave 22 years earlier, how do you feel now when you realize that this immensely powerful leader is your brother? [Discuss.]

The Bible tells us that Joseph's brothers were afraid of him. Close your eyes once more and listen to how Joseph practiced forgiveness and reassured his brothers, calming their fears.

- **Read from Genesis.** [Read Genesis 45:3-7.]

- **Discuss.** Now open your eyes and write [provide paper and pencils] down one thing you might want to say to your brother Joseph after he spoke those words to forgive you and help you to see God's hand in this broken relationship [3 minutes]. Now, please break into pairs and share what you wrote [3 minutes].

Summary.

- **Summary Statement.** We need each other. Even though relationships are hard, God can heal them and make them joyful and fruitful. As we are reconciled to God, all other relationships also begin to thrive. We have a relationship with God's Creation because we are a part of it. He wants us to see His beauty and sing His praise as we enjoy the glory and fruitfulness of His Creation. When we respect God's Creation, we honor Him and obey His command to take good care of it. This increases the blessings the earth can bring to our neighbors, which strengthens our relationships with them as well. God gave Joseph the wisdom to help a whole nation be in harmony with Creation even during a worldwide famine. So, as we see in Joseph's life, good relationships with God, people and God's earth are mutually beneficial – multiplying blessing and joy!

3. Who I Am: Healed Relationships

- **Example of Jesus.** Jesus initiated a relationship with a tax collector named Zacchaeus who oppressed lots of people by cheating them on their tax bills. This made people poorer and ruined his relationships with them. Listen to Luke 19:1-10 to see how a restored relationship with God affected his relationships with those he had bullied and robbed of their hard-earned wages:

    "Jesus was going through the city of Jericho. In Jericho there was a man named Zacchaeus. He was a wealthy, very important tax collector. He wanted to see who Jesus was, but he was too short to see above the crowd. He ran ahead to a place where he knew Jesus would come. He climbed a sycamore tree so he could see Jesus. When Jesus came to that place, he looked up and saw Zacchaeus in the tree. He said to him, 'Zacchaeus, hurry and come down! I must stay at your house today.' Zacchaeus came down quickly. He was pleased to have Jesus in his house. All the people saw this and began to complain, 'Look at the kind of man Jesus stays with. Zacchaeus is a sinner!' But Zacchaeus said to the Lord, 'I will give half of my money to the poor. If I have cheated anyone, I will pay that person back four times more!' Jesus said, 'Salvation has come to this house today. This man truly belongs to the family of Abraham. The Son of Man came to find lost people and save them.'"

    - What does this story teach us about how our relationships to God and to others are related? [Discuss.]
    - What did Jesus mean by 'This man truly belongs to the family of Abraham'?" [Discuss.]

    Jesus intended to restore both Zacchaeus' vertical and horizontal relationships. Harmony of all sorts is important to God. Why? Because He created us for intimacy with Him and each other. So, He works to heal all relationships that were damaged by sin.

- **Summary Scripture.** God made us to live in close community with each other. Listen to Genesis 2:18: "Then the Lord God said, 'It is not good for the man to be alone. I will make a helper who is right for him.'" As odd as it may sound, a healthy relationship with God was not the whole plan for Adam. Actually, part of closeness with God is closeness with the people He puts in our lives.

- **Summary Questions.** [Instruct students to give a thumbs up/down sign or shout out yes/no.]
    (1) Should we give up on relationships when things get hard? *No*
    (2) Should we follow Joseph's example by forgiving those who hurt us? *Yes*
    (3) Is God able to bring good out of the evil we do to each? *Yes*
    (4) Do you always know God's good purpose when bad things happen? *No*
    (5) Does a healthy relationship with God lead to healthy relationships with people and his world? *Yes*

(6) Does God want you to live in harmony with His world, caring for it and enjoying it? *Yes*

(7) Does it please God when we give up on broken relationships? *No*

Assign Homework.

- **Option A.** Memorize Genesis 50:20 and write it on a card and place it where you will see it every day. Write down three times when this verse came true in your own life.

- **Option B.** Go to someone who has hurt you and let them know you forgive them, are praying for them, and want what is best for them. Share how God has brought good out of the pain and that you want your relationship to be healed.

Closing Prayer. [If time is short, pray for the students. Otherwise, ask students to pray in pairs or small groups.] Students, please silently ask God to heal any relationships that are broken. [Give students 1-2 minutes to pray in silence, then close with a prayer for joyful and peaceful relationships with Him, people and the rest of His Creation.]

4. Who I Am: Pain that Matures

Supplies. Clock/watch with second hand or timer/stopwatch that records seconds as well as minutes.

FIRST HALF – 45 minutes

Review Previous Lesson's Homework. [Teacher has each adult lead a small group of students in sharing how their homework went. Adults record who did their homework as credit toward graduation.]

Share the title of today's lesson and how it fits into the course as a whole. [Review with students the "Opportunity Makers Overview" from the Appendix to remind them of how today's lesson connects to what they have been learning. For example, remind them of the Identity Statement (for lessons 1-5) or Purpose Statement (for lessons 6-12) and the truths from previous lessons. If possible, show these things on the whiteboard as well.]

Opening Prayer. [Pray.]

Student Activity.

- **Explain.** I need four boys and four girls who like to play sports to come up front to do an exercise. [Bring the eight students to a wall with nothing up against it before explaining further. Show them the Image of Wall Sitting in the Appendix so they understand what you want them to do or better yet: do it yourself!] I'd like to ask two boys and two girls to sit against this wall with no chair for as long as you can while the rest of us watch quietly.

- **Do.** [Demonstrate it yourself or show the Appendix photo which illustrates it. Then have the four students sit against the wall in silence while you or another adult record the length of time for each person. Add the four times together for a grand total.] Now, I'd like the next four students to do the same thing. [While this second foursome does the same timed exercise, have your most enthusiastic adult cheer them on the entire time, telling them how good they're doing and encouraging them to not give up. When the students start to get tired, the coach should get the whole class to clap their hands and cheer. If you're able to bring in a real sports coach for this role, that would be even better. Add their four times together as before.]

- **Debrief.**
    a. [Ask all eight students the following question.]
    What you did looked easy to us who were watching; was it? [Let them answer.]

Where did it hurt and how strongly did it burn? [Let them answer.]

b. [Ask the *first* four students the following question.]

How did our silence make you feel and do you think an encouraging coach would have helped you go longer? [Discuss.]

c. [Share the total times of the first and second groups with the class, then ask the *second* four students the following question.]

Did the cheering help you go longer and how can other people's voices improve what your own muscles do? [Discuss.]

d. [If you were able to bring in a real sports coach for this role, ask him or her the following question.]

Have you ever seen your lowest skilled players grow into your best players? [Let him or her answer.] What role does the combination of an encouraging coach and difficult workouts have in transforming new recruits into good athletes? [Let him or her answer.]

Teach the Truth and Lie.

- **Transition.** We just saw how the encouragement of a mentor can help us endure challenges, but do you ever feel like God is absent in your trials? We are tempted to believe that, but it's a big lie. God is certainly present when He *seems* most absent. As we see in Isaiah 63:9:

    "When they suffered, he suffered also.

    He sent his own angel to save them.

    Because of his love and kindness, the Lord saved them.

    Since long ago he has picked them up and carried them."

    Not only is He lovingly present, but He helps to carry our load – and us as well! We assume He's absent because of the pain we feel, but this verse assures us that He is right next to us feeling our pain along with us and helping us to grow through it. When someone learns to skydive, an experienced coach is attached to their back when they jump out of the airplane. Imagine it is you. Even with an expert to guide you, it's still scary to step off of a perfectly good airplane and fall like a rock to the earth. It's intensely loud and fast and windy. Any mistake could be fatal. At first, there's nothing slowing you down from a deadly impact onto the hard ground you're hurtling toward. But at just the right time, your invisible coach skillfully pulls the cord to open the parachute, maneuvers you to the landing zone, and helps you land smoothly. You *really* don't have to worry about much, but you *can* worry if you choose – especially if you forget there's an expert on your back! Same with God. You

4. Who I Am: Pain that Matures

may forget He's there, but that doesn't change the fact that He's guiding and protecting you, experiencing the same turbulent weather along with you. He's looking out for your good and preparing you for a fruitful future.

- **Read the Truth and Lie.** Today's entire lesson is built upon this biblical truth. Please read it aloud with me [from whiteboard or poster on wall where students can be reminded of the topic throughout the lesson].
  - ➢ **Truth about my identity: God's loving presence in my trials can produce beautiful fruit in my life.** When I realize that God shares my sorrows, He strengthens me and shapes my character. Even through my hardships, God is working for my good.
  - ➢ **Lie about my identity: My sufferings prove that God doesn't care about me.** Being cursed and alone makes me bitter and hopeless.

- **Explain.** Depending on how you react to suffering, it can break you or strengthen you. Trials can make you bitter or build resilience. It all depends on your outlook, your attitude. If you embrace the truth that a good God is in control and is looking out for your good, then you'll have confident hope that all will work out well for you in the end. Take the long view. In 100 years, will today's crisis matter? It may not even matter a year, month or week from now. What really matters to God is *who* you are becoming in the process. He is determined to make you like His Son Jesus, whereas making you 100% comfortable is less important to him. [Explain the truth further in your own words if necessary.]

- **Support with Scripture.** Listen to Romans 5:3-5:

    "And we also have joy with our troubles because we know that these troubles produce patience. And patience produces character, and character produces hope. And this hope will never disappoint us, because God has poured out his love to fill our hearts. God gave us his love through the Holy Spirit, whom God has given to us."

  So, as with Joseph, God uses suffering to shape you, to prepare you for bigger responsibilities ahead. And yet, He also shares your every sorrow, pouring out His love into your heart through the Holy Spirit.

- **Illustrate.** [Show students the Image of Grape Vine with Fruit in the Appendix.] Should the farmer let this grape vine get bigger every year so that it bears more and more fruit? [Discuss.]

  Actually, a grape vine will bear more fruit if it is cut way back. It's called pruning. Jesus actually used this illustration for our lives with Him. He said [John 15:1-2,5]:

    "I am the true vine; my Father is the gardener. He cuts off every branch of mine that does not produce fruit. And he trims and cleans every branch that produces fruit so that it will produce even more fruit.

I am the vine, and you are the branches. If a person remains in me and I remain in him, then he produces much fruit. But without me he can do nothing".

So, who are we in the story? [Discuss.]

[Hint: branches.]

And who gets pruned? [Discuss.]

[Hint: We do.]

Ouch! Yes, trials that God allows are not pleasant, but they can help us bear more fruit as we stay close to Jesus. He said we are as close to Him as a grape branch is to the vine it's connected to. We are tempted to think that God is absent when we suffer, but that's actually when He is closest to us. As Psalm 34:18 promises,

"The Lord is close to the brokenhearted. He saves those whose spirits have been crushed."

In fact, that very intimacy with God is what sustained Joseph. Genesis 49:22 says:

"Joseph is like a grape vine that produces much fruit. He is like a healthy vine watered by a spring."

It's surprising that Jacob used this grape vine image to describe his son Joseph many generations before Jesus used it to describe us. Actually, since he was very familiar with the book of Genesis, Jesus may have been thinking about Joseph when He used the grape vine illustration. Both passages reveal that the key to a healthy and fruitful grape branch is staying connected to the source of life. For Jesus, that was the vine. For Jacob, it was a spring that brought life. Both show that intimacy with God makes the difference between being fruitful and being shriveled by suffering. The secret is to receive God's loving embrace in the middle of the pain.

Example of Joseph.

- **Transition.** So, we learned from the words of Jacob and Jesus that embracing God's presence in pain is the key to a fruitful life. Godly character is part of the fruit God wants to produce in you through the difficulties of life. If you have the right attitude to suffering, it can powerfully shape you for good. God can use it transform you into a much better person. Let's look at Joseph's character before and after he suffered.

- **Read from Genesis.** [Read Genesis 37:5-9.]

- **Discuss.** When Joseph was 17 years old and his brothers already hated him, but he told his dreams to them anyway. His arrogance infuriated them. So, they plotted to kill him until Reuben convinced them to make some money by enslaving him instead. Then after 13 years as a slave and prisoner, he was suddenly given a huge opportunity for leadership and power that looked a lot like the dreams he had as a child. Was he still a boastful, self-centered person or did his life now revolve around serving others? [Discuss.]

4. Who I Am: Pain that Matures

What are some of Joseph's actions that show he had become a person of much stronger character than the boastful kid he used to be?

[Hints:]

- He used his high position to serve others rather than himself.
- He was diligent in leading a team to prepare well for the famine.
- He was faithful to distribute the food wisely.
- He did not seek revenge, but rather was generous and forgiving to brothers who had betrayed him.
- He did not gloat about his early dreams coming true.

During many setbacks over 13 long years, Joseph leaned on God for strength and believed that God was working for his good even when his present life looked hopeless.

Closing Prayer. [Thank God for key biblical insights uncovered during the lesson.]

SECOND HALF – 45 minutes

Opening Prayer. [Pray.]

Re-read Truth and Lie.

> - **Truth about my identity: God's loving presence in my trials can produce beautiful fruit in my life.** When I realize that God shares my sorrows, He strengthens me and shapes my character. Even through my hardships, God is working for my good.
> - **Lie about my identity: My sufferings prove that God doesn't care about me.** Being cursed and alone makes me bitter and hopeless.

Imagination Exercise.

- **Directions.** Put yourself into the story. You are Joseph and it is 13 years after you were thrown in a pit, taken from your father, from your country and enslaved. When it seemed like it couldn't get worse, it did. You were falsely accused and thrown into a worse pit: a dungeon. You helped someone who promised to help you in return, but he forgot all about you. But somehow, you never let this downward spiral of suffering crush your spirit. You have no idea that tomorrow the king will call you to his palace to interpret his two dreams and that your world will be turned upside down. But even in this dungeon of darkness, you've grown in strength and hope. How? It doesn't even seem possible.

- **Read from Genesis.** Your secret is recorded in Genesis 49:24-25. These are words of blessing your father spoke about you before he died: "His arms are made strong. He gets his power from the Mighty God of Jacob. He gets his strength from the Shepherd, the Rock of Israel. Your father's God helps you." If found in Joseph's shoes, most people would have been completely devastated rather than strengthened.

- **Discuss.** Here's a question I'd like you to think about quietly, then write down your answer: What helped you draw strength from God rather than become bitter towards God? [Repeat the question and write it on the whiteboard. Give them two minutes in silence to think about this question and write down their answers, then discuss with the whole class.]

Summary.

- **Summary Statement.** If you have the right attitude toward suffering, it can powerfully shape you for good. If you respond to trials with anger, you will become bitter and hopeless. On the other hand, God's loving presence in pain can produce beautiful fruit in your life – including godly character and the growth of God's gifts in you.

If you believe that God is near in your suffering, you – like Joseph – can learn to lean on God for strength and be encouraged as He shares in your pain. You'll gain confidence that He is working for your good and preparing you for bigger responsibilities ahead. You may even become grateful for how God has shaped you through suffering!

- **Example of Jesus:** Jesus shows us that God is not immune to pain, but rather willingly enters our pain in order to heal us. We see this when his friend Lazarus dies. [Read John 11:32-36.] Jesus joins Mary in grieving for her brother. Although Jesus raises Lazarus from the dead, He first takes time to feel the pain – deeply. Jesus wept. His tears were for Mary, for Martha, for His own sadness over our broken world, brimming with plagues of sin and death. Jesus weeps with *you* too, sharing your sorrow. He even suffered and died – willingly – so that we can be raised to new life – spiritually now and physically later. On that great day, He will wipe every tear from our eyes and make all things new! So, Jesus is the ultimate proof that suffering will not have the last word. We are not alone in our pain. No indeed. This good news is beautifully revealed in one of the Bible's name for Jesus: "Emmanuel." It means exactly what sustained Joseph during his 13 years of trials: "God with us."

- **Summary Scripture.** Let's read Romans 8:28, 31-32:

    "We know that in everything God works for the good of those who love him. They are the people God called, because that was his plan….If God is for us, then no one can defeat us. God let even his own Son suffer for us. God gave his Son for us all. So with Jesus, God will surely give us all things."

    Jesus giving His life for us is our once-for-all proof that God is for us and bears our sorrows. These verses assure us that God works for our good – even through the worst things that happen to us. He's that good and that powerful. In fact, the longer you live, you will look back on more and more difficult experiences and see how they did you more good than harm. You may become truly glad and grateful for some of the hardest seasons of your life. Please raise your hand if that has already happened to you at your young age. [Pause.]

    Would someone who raised their hand be willing to share what difficult experience you are now grateful for and how God brought good into your life through it? [Discuss for a few minutes if they are willing to share.]

- **Summary Questions.** [Instruct students to give a thumbs up/down sign or shout out yes/no.]

    (1) Does suffering show us that God doesn't care? *No*

    (2) When we suffer, does God suffer with us? *Yes*

    (3) Do trials prove that we are being cursed or punished? *No*

    (4) Will God work out everything for our good in the end? *Yes*

    (5) Should we give up hope when we don't understand why we suffer? *No*

(6) Will we look back on our lives and see the good fruit that came from times of "pruning"? *Yes*

(7) Does the suffering of Jesus give us eternal hope of freedom from sin and death? *Yes*

(8) Is the character He is shaping in us worth enduring the trials that help to form it? *Yes*

(9) Can our response to suffering make us either bitter or better? *Yes*

Assign Homework.

- **Option A.** Talk with someone whose relationship with God you admire. Ask them to tell you about a hard time that God used to shape their character.

- **Option B.** This week, encourage someone who is going through a hard time and share some of what you learned today.

- **Option C.** Look back on a hard time you went through and look for how God was present and working for your good. Write the story down and share it with someone.

Closing Prayer. [If time is short, pray for the students. Otherwise, ask students to pray in pairs or small groups. Pray about a personal challenge you're having to model for your students being vulnerable with God and asking for help. Pray for your students to experience God's presence in suffering then ask the class to pray silently about any current struggles they're going through.] He loves you and wants to hear from you about what you are going through. Even though God already knows your struggles, He desires to hear your heart. Be honest with God about how hard it is. Ask that His presence gives you strength.

5. Who I Am: Reflecting God

Supplies. Potted tree, bag of beans or rice, mirror, picture of sun and moon from Appendix.

FIRST HALF – 45 minutes

Review Previous Lesson's Homework. [Have each adult lead a small group of students in sharing how their homework went. Adults record who did their homework as credit toward graduation.]

Share the title of today's lesson and how it fits into the course as a whole. [Review with students the "Opportunity Makers Overview" from the Appendix to remind them of how today's lesson connects to what they have been learning. For example, remind them of the Identity Statement (for lessons 1-5) or Purpose Statement (for lessons 6-12) and the truths from previous lessons. If possible, show these things on the whiteboard as well.]

Opening Prayer. [Pray.]

Student Activity.

- **Explain.** [Have students draw a tree or large plant. Provide paper and pencils and show them the tree you want them to draw. Best to worst options are: large and beautiful tree they can see from where they sit, large potted plant you bring inside the classroom, small plant you put on the table a table so all can see, picture of a huge tree, or imagine a large tree.]

- **Do.** [Give students 5 minutes to draw the tree, asking them to capture as much of the beauty and details of the tree as they can. Allow 10 minutes total including setup, instructions, giving supplies, and drawing.]

- **Debrief.** Ask students:
    a. Is your picture a good reflection of the original tree? [Discuss.]
    b. How is your picture like the actual tree? [Discuss.]
    c. How is your picture unlike the real tree? [Discuss.]

    [Hints to give if students get stuck:]

ALIKE	UNALIKE
It is pretty.	It is not alive.
It reminds you of a real tree.	It is unable to bear fruit for people and animals.

It was created by someone.	You can't climb it.
It gives happiness.	It is flat.
It is valuable.	No animals can play or live in it.
It is drawn on paper made from a tree.	It doesn't give shade.
	It can't be used to build a house or a fire.
	It's not alive.

List several of students' ideas on a whiteboard using two columns (1) alike and (2) unalike.

Teach the Truth and Lie.

- **Transition.** Your pictures are like the real tree in big ways, but also unalike the real tree in important ways. The same is true between you and God; some character traits about God are his alone. Other things about God he wants us to copy. For example, we can't create a whole new world, but God has put us in charge of his world to take care of it and to create new things out of the good things he has already made. When we do that, we are like the pictures of the trees you drew - we look like the original, but not exactly.

- **Read the Truth and Lie.** Today's entire lesson is built upon this biblical truth. Please read it aloud with me [from whiteboard or poster on wall where students can be reminded of the topic throughout the lesson].

    ➢ **Truth about my identity: I am a reflection of God as I cultivate His earth and manage it wisely.** My life must show the world what God is like. I do this well as I become more and more like His Son Jesus.

    ➢ **Lie about my identity: I am just another animal which has evolved by chance.** I have no special identity or role. I am only dust that will return to the earth and be no more.

- **Explain.** If your parents ask you to look after the house while they're away, they expect you to do what they would do. You must represent them well and take good care of it. They would expect you to not make it dirty and not let bugs and thieves in. But they'd be even happier if you made it better – like sweeping the floor, making the bed, or cooking a tasty dinner. [Explain the truth further in your own words if necessary.]

- **Support with Scripture.** Here is a Bible verse that comes right after God created the world in Genesis and right before he created the first man and woman. Let's read Genesis 1:26-28: 'Then God said, 'Let us make human beings in our image and likeness. And let them rule over the fish in the sea and the birds in the sky. Let them rule over the tame animals, over all the earth and over all the small crawling animals on the earth.' So God created human beings in his image. In the image of God he created them. He created them male and

5. Who I Am: Reflecting God

female. God blessed them and said, "Have many children and grow in number. Fill the earth and be its master. Rule over the fish in the sea and over the birds in the sky. Rule over every living thing that moves on the earth. "From what this scripture tells us, how are we supposed to reflect God?" [Discuss.]

- **Illustrate.** God gave us the job of cultivating the earth and managing it wisely for him. [Repeat that sentence.] We don't always do a good job at this, but let's look at an example. [Choose one of the following two examples.]

Example 1: See verse 28: 'fill the earth and be its master.'

What are some of the things people have 'filled the earth' with using trees?

   [Hints… Give students as needed:]
   - maple syrup | houses | boats | furniture | the chair you're sitting on | the pencil in your hand | toy | mulch.

These are all different ways people have obeyed this command from God.

Example 2: Notice that verse 26 says we should 'rule over the tame animals.'

What are several ways people have ruled wisely over dogs? What things have people trained dogs to do?"

   Hints…as needed:]
   - trained to hunt | guide blind people | pull sleds over snow | find lost people or hidden drugs | go to the bathroom outside | protect us | race | be companions | entertain us.

Example of Joseph.

- **Transition.** Please raise your hand if you're learning for the first time that you were meant to cultivate and manage God's earth….Think back to the story of Joseph. How did he help the king of Egypt and the whole country? [Discuss.]

   [Hint:]
   - He advised that for seven years they were to save up some of the food they grew so everyone would have food to eat during the coming seven years of hunger. Then he worked to help people follow his plan.

- **Read from Genesis.** [Read Genesis 41: 33 - 40, 46 - 49.]

- **Discuss.** How did Joseph reflect God - showing people what God is like?"
  [Share some of the following teaching points.] Joseph reflected God as he…
  - Showed God's love by providing the food they needed to live.
  - Showed God's wisdom and power by solving a huge problem that affected the whole world.

- Did excellent work like God whose work of creating the world was "very good" [Genesis 1:31]. Imagine how much careful work it took to store up seven years' worth of food for an entire country!
- Did what he promised; he was worthy of trust just like God who is always faithful.
- Shaped the future for the good of all.
- Helped people work together to do good.
- Ruled next to the king over the whole land. Even though he was a slave and prisoner for 13 years, he never forgot that he was created to be one of God's leaders on earth.

Closing Prayer. [Thank God for key biblical insights uncovered during the lesson.]

5. Who I Am: Reflecting God

SECOND HALF – 45 minutes

Opening Prayer. [Pray.]

Re-read Truth and Lie.

> ➢ **Truth about my identity: I am a reflection of God as I cultivate His earth and manage it wisely.** My life must show the world what God is like. I do this well as I become more and more like His Son Jesus.

> ➢ **Lie about my identity: I am just another animal which has evolved by chance.** I have no special identity or role. I am only dust that will return to the earth and be no more.

Imagination Exercise.

- **Directions.** Part of Joseph's plan was for the king to appoint officers over the land to help Joseph store and guard the grain. As we read Genesis 41:34-35, close your eyes and imagine that you are one of these officers the king appoints!

- **Read from Genesis.** Read Genesis 41:34-35.

- **Discuss.** As leaders working on Joseph's team, all of you must figure out how to store grain for your own city. [Breaks class into trios and give each group one of these city names from ancient Egypt: Memphis, Thebes, Alexandria, Amarna, Abydos, Hermopolis, Crocodilopolis, Elephantine, and Kom Ombo.]
[Open bag of beans or rice and gives a handful to each student.]

Imagine that you are meeting together right now as city leaders to solve these two problems:

    Problem 1: Thieves are stealing some of the grain you are storing.

    Problem 2: Insects are eating some of it.

What should be done to solve these two problems?

[Ask students to take a minute to write down possible solutions individually, then discuss them as a city team for five minutes.]

[Regather the class and ask each city team to share their best solution to one of the problems.]

[Optional…] What do you want to learn from Joseph to do your job well? [Discuss.]

Summary.

- **Summary Statement.** We learned today that God created us to be His reflections here on earth. We cultivate and manage God's earth so that its blessings can be developed for everyone. The way we work together to solve problems also reflects the wisdom and power of God. As everything God created was good, so we should do all our work with excellence, making beautiful and helpful things that bless others. While Joseph is a good example of reflecting God, Jesus gives us the ultimate example of being like His Father. In fact, becoming more and more like Jesus is God's goal for each of us [Romans 8:29).]

- **Example of Jesus.** Jesus reflects our Heavenly Father perfectly [John 14:7, Colossians 1:15]!

    When we look at any part of Jesus' life, we learn who God is…

    - When we see that Jesus became human, we know that God and empties himself to serve rebels like us.
    - When Jesus teaches about the Father, we know that God wants us to know Him.
    - When Jesus heals the sick, we know that God is filled with compassion for our weaknesses.
    - When Jesus dies for us, we know that God loves us enough to send his Son to lay down His life to free us from our sins and to adopt us as His children.
    - When Jesus rose from the dead, we know that God has won the victory over death and will make all things new.
    - As we put our trust in Jesus and follow Him, we become more and more like Him. As His reflections, the world can look at us to see what God is like."

- **Summary Scripture.** Listen to Isaiah 60:1-3:

    "Jerusalem, get up and shine. Your light has come. The glory of the Lord shines on you. Darkness now covers the earth. Deep darkness covers her people. But the Lord shines on you, and people see his glory around you. Nations will come to your light. Kings will come to the brightness of your sunrise."

    "Where does the light of the moon come from?"

    [Discuss. Use a mirror to reflect light onto the wall or shows students the image of the moon from the Appendix.]

    We are like the moon: our light is real and beautiful, but its source is not from us but from the Lord Jesus who shines into the world through us as we cultivate His earth and manage it wisely.

- **Summary Questions.** [Instruct students to give a thumbs up/down sign or shout out yes/no.]

    (1) Can we become exactly like God in every way? *No.* (There is only one God – only He knows everything and can save us from our sins.)

    (2) Can we become more like God in important ways? *Yes*

    (3) Has God put us in charge of His earth like the king put Joseph in charge of Egypt? *Yes*

    (4) Is it okay for us to do whatever we want with the earth? *No.*

    (We must cultivate and manage it wisely in a way that pleases God and blesses people.)

5. Who I Am: Reflecting God

(5) Is making plans for a better future for our community part of our job? *Yes*

(6) Does God use people to provide for the world's needs? *Yes*

(7) Is God pleased when we do sloppy work? *No* We must do good work to reflect God.

(8) Can we become like God without becoming like Jesus? *No* We must keep our eyes on Jesus and follow Him to become like the Father.

Assign Homework.

- **Option A.** List all the ways you want to become more like Jesus and Joseph. Choose one to work on this week and ask someone to help you and pray for you.

- **Option B.** Even if it is very small, how can you cultivate and manage a part of God's earth for him?
[Ideas:] plant a garden | help dad or mom with younger kids | make something beautiful | useful to help someone else.

Closing Prayer. [If time is short, pray for the students. Otherwise, ask students to pray in pairs or small groups.] Pray for God to use you, to make you more like Jesus, and for others to be drawn to God's light by looking at His reflection in you.

6. Why I'm Here: God's Plan

Supplies. Drawing paper and colored pencils if available.

FIRST HALF – 45 minutes

Review Previous Lesson's Homework. [Have each adult lead a small group of students in sharing how their homework went. Adults record who did their homework as credit toward graduation.]

Share the title of today's lesson and how it fits into the course as a whole. [Review with students the "Opportunity Makers Overview" from the Appendix to remind them of how today's lesson connects to what they have been learning. For example remind them of the Identity Statement (for lessons 1-5) or Purpose Statement (for lessons 6-12) and the truths from previous lessons. If possible, show these things on the whiteboard as well.]

Opening Prayer. [Pray.]

Student Activity.

- **Explain.** Draw a picture of the place you most want to go with your family.
  [Provide paper/pen and allow 5 minutes.]

- **Do.** [Have students break into pairs for two minutes and explain their picture and share why they want to go to the place they drew. Then re-gather.]

- **Debrief.** What would it take to make the trip to your perfect place possible?" [Discuss.]
  What are all the steps your family would have to take? What are all the plans that would have to be made?
  [List on whiteboard or large piece of paper if possible.]
    [Hints…]
    - Learn about the destination and decide fun things you want to do there.
    - Learn about cost and save money.
    - Arrange for transportation, food, and lodging – on the way, while you're there and on the way back home.
    - Parents may have to take off from work.
    - Arrange for people, animals and plants staying behind.
    - Ask other people to help with other responsibilities your family normally has.

Notice how much careful planning it takes to have a great trip!

[Write it where they can see it and then repeat it out loud.]

Teach the Truth and Lie.

- **Transition.** "Who like surprises? [Raise hands.] I have good news for you!

- **Read the Truth and Lie.** Today's entire lesson is built upon this biblical truth. Please read it aloud with me [from whiteboard or poster on wall where students can be reminded of the topic throughout the lesson].

  ➢ **Truth about my purpose: God has a good plan for my life** – to join in his work of making all things right and good. My life and work are to be a small preview of the day when God's Kingdom comes on earth as it is in heaven. Then my cooperation with God will increase – to the point of even reigning with Him!

  ➢ **Lie about my purpose: My life has no meaning.** I come from nothing and will go to nothing. I am nothing. The world is no better because I exist. With no reason to serve others, my only purpose is to take whatever I can for myself.

- **Explain.** [Explain the truth further in your own words if necessary.] God is planning a huge surprise for you. He has carefully planned out a trip for you. The trip is your life. Even though it includes some difficult and dangerous parts, you can trust that the plan for this trip is good because it was designed by a good God who loves you more than you can imagine. Like planning wisely for a trip to your favorite place, God has chosen the people and the places and events in your life for your good – even if it doesn't all make sense to you yet. The best part of God's plan for your journey through life is that He goes with you! I fact, He even lets you share in His important work of leading his world into what is right and good. The Bible says in 1 Corinthians 3:9:

  "We are God's co-workers."

What an amazing surprise! We get to work with God to care for the world and everything in it. Wow! We have a big job. God could do everything himself, but he enjoys letting us be his little helpers. This was His plan from the very beginning. In Genesis, God let Adam and – the first person he created – give names to all the animals. That must have been fun!

- **Support with Scripture.** [Read Genesis 2:19-20.]

- **Illustrate.** God put Adam in charge of watching over the animals and cultivating the plants. As descendants of Adam, we now have the job of assisting God in his work here, including helping the earth bear fruit to bless people as well as introducing people to God who can forgive their sins and heal their broken relationships.

6. Why I'm Here: God's Plan

Joseph – and Jesus, best of all – shows us that we must lead by serving people – which often requires lots of careful planning like getting ready for a trip to your favorite place. So, it turns out that God's plan for you is connected to God's plan for the world. He wants you to work with Him to help make things right around here. God can use us to heal broken relationships and call them to restored relationships with God. That is a hugely important purpose that God has given us – sharing in His own purpose of restoring all things to fit His plan. Now that's a big surprise, especially when we sometimes feel small or wonder if our loves matter. The next time you are tempted to believe that lie, remember that "we are God's co-workers"!

Example of Joseph.

- **Transition.** While being enslaved and imprisoned in Egypt for 13 years, Joseph didn't know how his suffering fit in with God's plan for him and the world. He could have been angry with God for allowing his brothers to sell him to the Ishmaelite's who took him away from his family and homeland to a country where he'd never been and didn't even know the language people spoke. He could have lost hope and even kill himself. Joseph probably had moments of doubt, but he clung to God in trust and hope. This close relationship during 13 long, hard years shaped Joseph into a godly person and prepared him to be used by God in a powerful way. Four times in Genesis 19, the Bible tells us that "the Lord was with Joseph" – twice while he was a slave and twice while he was a prisoner. In the hardest times of his life, God was with him and helped him to focus on serving others very well – both in his daily life as well as in sharing the meaning of dreams. Only by turning to God's 'strengthening presence' with us and His plan for the world can we look past or own problems to serve others with God's love.

Thirteen years of faithfully working with God in the shadows prepared him to work with God in the spotlight. When the king of Egypt had a dream that troubled him, he asked Joseph for help. Listen to his conversation with the King. [Read Genesis 41:15-16.] Notice that Joseph quickly pointed out that he could not give the meaning on his own – he was working together with God just like the truth in this lesson states. God shows the meaning of the dream and Joseph shares it with the King.

Remember that God's plan is to share his work of caring for the world and its people with us – his little helpers. He could have made Egypt's story go a different way, like preventing the famine altogether or letting Egypt suffer through it alone, or by telling the King directly what he should do. Instead, he used one of His people who looked like a nobody to save the entire world from starvation. God has big plans for us to work alongside him to bless the world. After Joseph shared the meaning of the dream to the King, the Bible says…

- **Read from Genesis.** [Read Genesis 41:38-40.]

    "So, even the King saw that Joseph was working together with God! It was obvious that Joseph was close to God and was given God's wisdom.

Do you remember what Joseph did after the King put him in charge?

[Hopefully a student will answer: "he planned and organized teams to collect extra food during the seven 'lean' years."]

Joseph had learned as a child how God had put Adam and Eve in charge of the earth and now, he was taking on that role of cultivating the earth to bless the world's people. With God's wisdom, he made careful plans that were a lot more detailed and harder to carry out than the planning needed to visit your favorite place. His cooperation with God saved millions of lives – including his own family members who came to Egypt to buy some of the grain Joseph had stored. So, God's plan was finally revealed. Joseph could now see the purpose God had in him being forcibly taken to Egypt and enslaved. The years of learning to work hard and trust God in the prison prepared him to successfully complete a big job with God's wisdom and strength. Imagine the joy he felt knowing that God used him to feed millions of starving people! God has an important plan for *you* too, which involves teamwork with him to bless others.

Closing Prayer. [Thank God for key biblical insights uncovered during the lesson.]

6. Why I'm Here: God's Plan

SECOND HALF – 45 minutes

Opening Prayer. [Pray.]

Re-read Truth and Lie.

- ➢ **Truth about my purpose: God has a good plan for my life** – to join in his work of making all things right and good. My life and work are to be a small preview of the day when God's Kingdom comes on earth as it is in heaven. Then my cooperation with God will increase – to the point of even reigning with Him!
- ➢ **Lie about my purpose: My life has no meaning.** I come from nothing and will go to nothing. I am nothing. The world is no better because I exist. With no reason to serve others, my only purpose is to take whatever I can for myself.

Imagination Exercise.

- **Read from Genesis.** [Read Genesis 41:40.]

- **Directions.** Pretend that you are the King and you've just appointed Joseph as your prime minister top assistant. Some people are grumbling because you appointed an imprisoned foreign slave as the second highest ruler in the whole country. So, to explain your reasons to the country, you are preparing for an interview with the Egypt Times newspaper. To have some notes to use in the interview, please write your answers to these three questions that the newspaper reporter sent you on a scroll.
  - What qualifies this imprisoned foreign slave to be the Prime Minister?
  - How did Joseph know the meaning of your dreams?
  - How do you know that he is telling the truth?

  [Give them two minutes to answer each of the three questions, then have them share their answers in pairs. Walk around and listen for some interesting answers that reinforce the lesson.]

- **Discuss.** [Have one student share their answer with the whole class – or three students who each address one of the questions.]

Summary.

- **Summary Statement.** God's plan for you is part of His plan for the whole world. You are invited into the joy of working together with God to accomplish His plan to make all things right and good in His world.

- **Example of Jesus.** Even more than Joseph, Jesus was in perfect tune with His Father's plan and thrived on carrying it out. He constantly followed God's plan to make things right on earth by healing the sick, teaching and showing who God is, and even sacrificing His life that we may live. He found great joy and soul nourishment in restoring all things to God.

- **Summary Scripture.** Jesus said in John 4:34: "My food is to do what the One who sent me wants me to do. My food is to finish the work that he gave me to do." Notice that Jesus got his joy, his soul nourishment from working together with His Father. So should we!

- **Summary Questions.** [Instruct students to give a thumbs up/down sign or shout out yes/no.]

    (1) Can we trust God's good plan for us even when it leads us through some difficult and dangerous days? *Yes*

    (2) Do years of trails prove that God has abandoned me? *No*

    (3) Is God's plan for you connected to His plan for the world? *Yes*

    (4) Does God do His work without us, so we don't mess it up? *No*

    (5) Does God enjoy involving His people in His work? *Yes*

    (6) Did Joseph lose hope in God when God's plan for his life got hard? *No*

    (7) Is it possible to look past our own troubles and find joy in serving others alongside the Lord? *Yes*

    (8) Did Joseph take all the credit for himself for telling the meaning of the King's dream? *No*

    (9) If God used an imprisoned foreign slave like Joseph to save the world from starvation, can He use me to do something special even if I feel very small? *Yes*

    (10) Does working with God automatically make it easy? *No* [Even though God gave Joseph strength and wisdom, planning for and storing grain in cities all over Egypt for 7 years was a long and complicated job.]

Assign Homework.

- **Option A.** Write down the story of a time you felt joy when helping people. What hints were there to show that God was working with you?

- **Option B.** Give your problems to God and ask Him to help you join Him in serving others.

- **Option C.** When you think about something good you've done, give God credit for helping you.

Closing Prayer. [If time is short, pray for the students. Otherwise, ask students to pray in pairs or small groups.] Express your trust in God and surrender to His good plan. Ask for strength to do good work and rely on God even when things are hard. Ask God to show you what he is doing in your neighborhood and give you an opportunity to serve Him.

[Lead class in closing prayer with Psalm 8:3-9.]

Please close your eyes and join me. "Dear Lord, like King David who wrote this psalm, we are amazed that you've entrusted us with such a big, important job…[Read Psalm 8:3-9 in prayer.] Amen.

7. Why I'm Here: God's Gifts

FIRST HALF – 45 minutes

Review Previous Lesson's Homework. [Have each adult lead a small group of students in sharing how their homework went. Adults record who did their homework as credit toward graduation.]

Share the title of today's lesson and how it fits into the course as a whole. [Review with students the "Opportunity Makers Overview" from the Appendix to remind them of how today's lesson connects to what they have been learning. For example remind them of the Identity Statement (for lessons 1-5) or Purpose Statement (for lessons 6-12) and the truths from previous lessons. If possible, show these things on the whiteboard as well.]

Opening Prayer. [Pray.]

Student Activity.

- **Explain.** We're going to break into trios [or larger groups if you have more than 24 students].
  You are the best robot designers in the world and your town [or neighborhood, or church, or school] has asked you to build an amazing robot to solve a big problem that the town has. Decide:
  (1) What problem your robot will work on.
  (2) What abilities you will give the robot.
  (3) How the town's robot will use the skills you give it to make life better in your town.

- **Do.** Take five minutes to discuss these three questions [display on whiteboard]. Choose one person to share your ideas with the class.

- **Debrief.** [Remind each trio to choose a spokesperson and give each group one minute each to share their plans with the class – up to eight minutes total for this sharing time.]
  - How would you feel if your robot decides to only help itself rather than the whole town? [Discuss.]
  - How would you feel if the robot doubts the abilities you had given it and decides to do nothing at all? [Discuss.]

Teach the Truth and Lie.

- **Transition.** Our relationships with God are a little bit like your robot's relationship to you.
- **Read the Truth and Lie.** Today's entire lesson is built upon this biblical truth. Please read it aloud with me [from whiteboard or poster on wall where students can be reminded of the topic throughout the lesson].

Opportunity Makers

- ➢ **Truth about my purpose: I must develop God's gifts.** My life and my gifts are not my own. I have received everything from God. He owns everything and expects me to use everything entrusted to me for His glory. So, I must develop and use these for God: my mind, body, soul, character, time, resources and relationships. God expects me to put these extremely valuable gifts to work to serve my community.

- ➢ **Lie about my purpose: I am empty-handed and have nothing to offer.** I am poor. I am a beggar. The government should help me. The little I do have is mine to spend on myself. I answer to no one; my life is my own. I can do whatever I want with my life. I can ignore my gifts or use them only for myself.

- **Explain.** Just like your robot has to answer to you because you made it, so we are accountable to God because He created us. He gave us a job to do and the abilities to get the job done. [Explain the truth further in your own words if necessary.]

- **Support with Scripture.** [Read Matthew 25:14-30. If there is extra time, print out several copies of Matthew 25:14-30 and underline each character's part for student volunteers to read in front of the class.]

- **Illustrate.** How is this story similar to our robot exercise? [Discuss.]

  What do you think of these three servants? [Discuss]

  Why do you think the master gives the first two servants more? [Discuss.]

  A robot may not be able to develop their skills, but when we use our skills, God gives us more. Think of your favorite soccer player and consider that there was a time that he or she could not even stand. Much less walk, run or make an amazing goal on the soccer field. As we use our gifts to serve our master and the world he loves, they grow stronger and more useful. But if we're lazy or selfish with God's gifts, we will miss the joyful opportunity of bigger responsibilities that God wants to entrust to us.

Example of Joseph.

- **Transition.** The same thing happened with Joseph. When he used God's gifts wisely, the king trusted him with the huge responsibility of helping an entire country through a long famine. Let's see some of the hard work that Joseph did to be faithful to his assignment.

- **Read from Genesis.** Recall that God had shown Joseph that in seven years there would be a massive food shortage and he had been given the huge job of helping an entire country get ready for that natural disaster. Here's what he did…. [Read Genesis 41:46-49.]

- **Discuss.** Storing up seven years' worth of food was a huge job.

  What made this job difficult job - requiring Joseph to use all of his God-given skills?

7. Why I'm Here: God's Gifts

How would this be a huge challenge?

[Hints…]

- It had never been done before.
- Many storage containers probably had to be built.
- He had to safeguard the food from rotting or being stolen by people or eaten by insects.
- He had to make sure people were setting aside enough each year for seven years.
- All of this required the teamwork of many people for many years – and you know how people like to fight!

Remember that the master in Jesus' parable said: "You did well. You are a good servant who can be trusted. You did well with small things so I will let you care for much greater things" [Matthew 25:21]. What prepared Joseph for such a big job? What are the small things he was faithful with that developed the skills he needed to get Egypt through a seven-year food shortage? [Discuss.]

[Hints…]

- He figured out how to run Potiphar's household and then the entire prison he was in. He had to be eager to learn new things then do his best work every time to earn the trust of those who were over him.
- Joseph didn't take credit for the gifts that God gave him. Instead, he acknowledges that God was the source of the interpretation of the dreams in the prison [Genesis 40:8] and in the palace [Genesis 41:16]. He wanted God to be praised rather than people saying how great Joseph was. This humility helped him focus on developing the skills to serve others rather than being selfish. As a co-worker with God, Joseph developed a skill for solving problems which was highly valued by Potiphar, the jailor, Pharaoh, all of Egypt and people of the surrounding countries who came to buy the food he had stored up – including his own family!

How would most people feel about using their gifts to serve others when they are enslaved or imprisoned for no good reason?

[Hints…]

- Many would only learn the skills needed to get revenge on those who enslaved them.
- Many would feel sorry for themselves while suffering wrongfully for 13 years.
- Many would do the minimum amount of work and do poor work to harm their oppressors.

Closing Prayer. [Thank God for key biblical insights uncovered during the lesson.]

SECOND HALF – 45 minutes

Opening Prayer.

Re-read Truth and Lie.

> - **Truth about my purpose: I must develop God's gifts.** My life and my gifts are not my own. I have received everything from God. He owns everything and expects me to use everything entrusted to me for His glory. So, I must develop and use these for God: my mind, body, soul, character, time, resources and relationships. God expects me to put these extremely valuable gifts to work to serve my community.
> - **Lie about my purpose: I am empty-handed and have nothing to offer.** I am poor. I am a beggar. The government should help me. The little I do have is mine to spend on myself. I answer to no one; my life is my own. I can do whatever I want with my life. I can ignore my gifts or use them only for myself.

Imagination Exercise.

- **Directions.** Put yourself into the story. Imagine that you are Joseph and right after you interpret the king's dream and suggest he appoint a leader to prepare for the coming food shortage, the king says this to you…

- **Read from Genesis.** [Genesis 41:39-44]

- **Discuss.** How did the king's words make you feel? [Discuss.]

As soon as you learn the king's court, which of these should you do? [Discuss.

[Hints…]

- Thank God for this opportunity to serve then share the happy news with your family.
- Go to look for the biggest and fanciest house and take it for yourself.
- Ask the king to host a huge party to show everyone how powerful and wonderful you are.

Is there a difference between what you *should* do and what you *would* do? [Discuss…]

What did Joseph actually do? Let's see. [Read Genesis 41:46-49.]

He got right to work to use his gifts to serve the good of all – not just himself. He travelled around the country to learn and plan and build teamwork with the people he would need to lead in the massive job of storing and guarding seven years' worth of food. He decided to use the huge amount of power that the king gave him to fulfill his purpose of preventing millions of people from starving. He did this to please God even more then the king. Just like Joseph, God gives you gifts that you will enjoy most when you use them to serve others. You might not feel like you have much, but you have more than you realize: body, mind, soul, character, time,

7. Why I'm Here: God's Gifts

resources, and relationships. Just like a future soccer star needs to learn how to walk first, I encourage you to develop these gifts of God now so that you are ready to be his coworker in bigger and bigger ways of blessing others as a leader who serves.

Summary.

- **Summary Statement.** Develop God's gifts and work hard daily to bless others with them. This will build trust that will open up even bigger opportunities to lead by serving. When you give credit to Gid and use your abilities to bless others more than yourself, God will fill you with the joy of being his coworker.

- **Example of Jesus.** Joseph's great example of saving the world from a food shortage points to Jesus who saved the world from separation from God. Even as the Son of God, as a young boy he had to learn to develop his mind and practice serving people through his human body. Luke 2:52 says:

  "Jesus continued to learn more and more and to grow physically. People liked him, and he pleased God."

  Even as a boy, Jesus was developing himself – not *for* himself but to serve God and people. He was preparing for history's biggest job of co-working with God to restore humanity and creation to God's original goodness. Although this led to His death on a cross, He considered "the joy set before him" as greater than the suffering that he endured. Like the servant in the parable who multiplied his master's investment, Jesus heard His Father say [Matthew 25:21]: "Come and share my happiness with me"

- **Summary Scripture.** This verse is an excellent summary of this lesson. Let's read 1 Peter 4:10:

  "God has shown you his grace in giving you different gifts. And you are like servants who are responsible for using God's gifts. So be good servants and use your gifts to serve each other."

- **Summary Questions.** [Instruct students to give a thumbs up/down sign or shout out yes/no.]

  (1) Should we take credit for the gifts God has given us? *No*

  (2) Will our abilities grow much stronger as we use them? *Yes*

  (3) Is it okay to ignore our talents because we are afraid or don't think they are worth much? *No*

  (4) Are our gifts intended to serve ourselves more than others? *No*

  (5) Will we be even happier when we use all we have to bless others? *No*

  (6) Does God have more important work for us to do with him than we can even imagine now? *Yes*

  (7) Is it important that we do excellent work every day to build a reputation of being reliable and trustworthy? *Yes*

Assign Homework.

- **Option A.** Make a list of all the gifts and abilities God has given you, including those related to your body, mind, soul, character, time, resources, and relationships. Take some time to think and write them down. Ask important people in your life – such as parents, grandparents, teachers, pastors and friends – what strengths they see in you.
- **Option B.** Choose three gifts from your list that you would like to focus on developing.
- **Option C.** Choose one way to use at least one of your gifts to serve others this week. Then make a habit to do this regularly.

Closing Prayer. [If time is short, pray for the students. Otherwise, ask students to pray in pairs or small groups.]

Dear Lord, please give us your strength to develop our gifts even in hard situations. Show us that like Joseph and Jesus experienced, you will use our difficult circumstances to bless many people. As we live out this lesson, we look forward to hearing you say to us: "You did well. You are a good servant who can be trusted. You did well with small things. So, I will let you care for much greater things. Come and share my happiness with me." Please fill us with the power of your Spirit until that final day. In Jesus' name we pray, amen.

8. Why I'm Here: Good Work

Supplies. One large pair of men's shoes and one large pair of women's shoes.

FIRST HALF – 45 minutes

Review Previous Lesson's Homework. [Have each adult lead a small group of students in sharing how their homework went. Adults record who did their homework as credit toward graduation.]

Share the title of today's lesson and how it fits into the course as a whole. [Review with students the "Opportunity Makers Overview" from the Appendix to remind them of how today's lesson connects to what they have been learning. For example, remind them of the Identity Statement (for lessons 1-5) or Purpose Statement (for lessons 6-12) and the truths from previous lessons. If possible, show these things on the whiteboard as well.]

Opening Prayer. [Pray.]

Student Activity.

- **Explain.** Show large pairs of adult shoes (at least one man's and one woman's pair) to the class. "Did you ever try walking around in your parent's shoes?"

- **Do.** [Give some or all students a chance to put on the large shoes you brought to class and take pictures of them with adult looks on their faces.]

- **Debrief.** When playing at home, did you ever put on adult shoes or use adult tools and pretend to work? If yes, please raise your hand. [Ask students with their hands raised]
  What kind of work did you pretend to do? [Make sure girls get a chance to answer as much as boys. Let a few share with the class.]
  Why do you think you pretended to work instead of pretending to do something else? [Discuss.]
    [Hints…]
    - Working gives us a sense of purpose since it helps other people.
    - Work involves creating or restoring things – both of which reflect God as we are designed to do.
    - We enjoy accomplishing things – both starting new things and finishing them.
    - Work is a great way to develop and use God's gifts as we saw in the previous lesson.

- Work is a place where we can experience the excellence we crave.
- Work can sometimes be a place where our most important relationships – with God, people, and creation – are strengthened.
- Work is where we can partner with God to develop his creation.

Teach the Truth and Lie.

- **Transition.** You don't have to be an adult or get paid to have the satisfaction of doing good work.

- **Read the Truth and Lie.** Today's entire lesson is built upon this biblical truth. Please read it aloud with me [from whiteboard or poster on wall where students can be reminded of the topic throughout the lesson].
  - **Truth about my purpose: Work is a good gift from God to bless others.** Working with excellence is a way to worship God and cooperate with Him to serve others. It helps me to imitate God who is a worker and it brings out the usefulness and beauty of His earth. The purpose of my work is to love my neighbors as Jesus commands which brings me joy.
  - **Lie about my purpose: Work is a curse or a burden.** I should do the minimum amount of work because I get paid so little and my supervisors are not good people. My work is meaningless and always frustrating.

- **Explain.** While work can be frustrating because we are broken people in a broken world, it can still be very fulfilling because it is a main way that we can imitate God. [Explain the truth further in your own words if necessary.]

- **Support with Scripture.** We know that work is a good gift from God because God was the original worker and He declared that His work was good – very good!

  Let's listen to Genesis 1:31:

  "God looked at everything he had made, and it was very good. Evening passed, and morning came. This was the sixth day." What God did next was amazing – He invited one kind of creature He had just created to start working alongside Him!

  Listen to Genesis 2:19 – 20a:

  "From the ground God formed every wild animal and every bird in the sky. He brought them to the man so the man could name them. Whatever the man called each living thing, that became its name. The man gave names to all the tame animals, to the birds in the sky and to all the wild animals."

Notice that God saw Adam's help as an important partnership. God created the creatures and invited Adam to create their names.

Why do you think God was so pleased to see one creature naming other creatures?" [Discuss.]

[Hints…]

- As God's reflections, this was the start of human partnering with God as manager of his world.
- God enjoys seeing us grow into our full potential.
- God enjoys seeing us further develop His creation and use His gifts.
- God – who is a community of Father, Son and Spirit – enjoys teamwork with us.

In the next Genesis passage, we see God giving Adam and Eve more creative work to do – caring for the garden, cultivating the earth's plants and animals, and building families and societies. These instructions are for all of us – not just for Adam and Eve. We have already seen how Joseph worked together with God to prevent millions of people from starving. Much later in human history, the Apostle Paul wrote that "we are God's fellow workers" [1 Corinthians 3:9a]. What an astounding privilege, honor, and joy!

- **Illustrate.** The way God shares his work with us is a little like a mother who helps her daughter mature into a capable adult. Since carrying her in her own womb, the mother cares about what is best for her daughter. At first the infant cannot do anything on her own. Whether teaching her to eat, helping her take her first steps, or helping her learn to read, the mother wants her daughter to become more and more able to take good care of herself and others. It would be a problem if at age ten she was still as helpless as a baby. Instead, the mother teaches and trains her daughter to become a mature adult, through ever increasing responsibilities in the family, and maybe even the family business where her unique abilities can add something unique. The mother appreciates whatever help the daughter contributes as her capabilities grow but is mostly excited to see how she is maturing as a person and as a leader who is a blessing and a good example to others. She can now make her own decisions – even very good ones – because she has become a lot like her mom.

In the same way, God is excited to see us grow up into mature daughters and sons whose lives reflect Him and are focused on His mission to His lost and suffering world. Sharing His heart for the world draws His children close to Him, an intimacy He deeply cherishes.

Example of Joseph.

- **Transition.** Family isn't always as nurturing as this picture of mother and daughter. Consider Joseph being sold into slavery by his own brothers! Imagine the pain of that betrayal. It would have broken Joseph's spirit if he was not clinging tightly to his heavenly Father for strength. The Bible doesn't tell us what Joseph was feeling after being thrown in a pit by his own brothers, sold to foreigners, taken to a strange country, then made to work without pay for someone whose language he didn't understand. At the end of his life, Joseph's father Jacob blessed him and gave us this hint about how Joseph survived and even thrived when his whole life was in an upheaval: "He gets his power from the Mighty God of Jacob. He gets strength from the Shepherd, the Rock of Israel. Your Father's God helps you." [Genesis 49:24-25] Without the anchor of his identity as a cherished child of God, Joseph would not have had the confidence and energy to do excellent work in the following passage.

- **Read from Genesis.** As we read, listen for words that are repeated. [Read Genesis 39:1-6.] Then after a false accusation resulted in Joseph being imprisoned – an even worse situation than being a slave. Did he let that break him and strangle his hope? Let's see…[Read Genesis 39: 21-23.]

- **Discuss.** What are some words that are repeated in these scenes from Joseph's time as a slave and a prisoner? [Discuss. Display the passage or reread if necessary.]
    - "The Lord was with Joseph." – mentioned four times
    - Joseph was "successful" – mentioned three times
    - Joseph was "put in charge" – mentioned four times.
    - People surrounding Joseph were "blessed" – mentioned two times

   What surprises you about how Joseph was living enslaved and imprisoned?

   How did Joseph's actions transform the places where he worked?

    [Hints…]
    - They were blessed.
    - His supervisors could focus on other things knowing that Joseph was responsible.
    - Potiphar's farm was more profitable.

   How did his supervisors react to Joseph's work?

    [Hints…]
    - They gave him additional responsibility.
    - They trusted him.
    - They were happy with him.
    - They saw that the Lord was with him.

   What kind of work must Joseph have been doing to cause his supervisors to respond like that?

[Hints…]

- He learned how to do lots of new tasks and found ways to do them better than expected.
- He did his very best and with a good attitude.
- Instead of doing the minimum required, he tried to be a maximum blessing to his supervisors.
- He treated people right every time.
- He did not waste time or materials, but rather worked with them efficiently to create value for his supervisors.
- He did all of this consistently so that he earned a reputation for responsibility and trustworthiness.

Joseph's remarkable work was rooted in his identity as a child of God and in his close relationship with God. He knew who he was – a son of God with an important job – not a slave or a prisoner. Since the one who lovingly created him values him immensely, it doesn't matter what others think. Yes, people still hurt him but God's love healed him. In his work in Potiphar's house and in his work in the prison, his success is connected with the fact that the Lord was with him. [Reread Genesis 39:3,23.]

Another part of Jacob's blessing over his son Joseph reads "Joseph is like a grapevine that produces much fruit. He is like a healthy vine watered by a spring" [Genesis 49:22]. This verse explains why Joseph was able to produce much fruit. The spring was the secret to the fruitful vine. Constant nourishment from below the surface enabled Joseph to thrive even in difficult circumstances. Because the Lord was with him, he saw himself as a co-worker with God to bless everyone and everything around him. Knowing that God himself does excellent work and put him where he was as God's representative, he brought good into very challenging workplaces. Not reacting to his outward circumstances, he chose to live from God's deep inner resources that flowed through him to bless others. Like Joseph, you can live from your identity as a child of God rather than feeling imprisoned by your present circumstances. Like Adam and Eve cultivating God's garden, you are called to work with God to make everything around you better.

Closing Prayer. [Thank God for key biblical insights uncovered during the lesson.]

SECOND HALF – 45 minutes

Opening Prayer.

Re-read Truth and Lie.

> - **Truth about my purpose: Work is a good gift from God to bless others.** Working with excellence is a way to worship God and cooperate with Him to serve others. It helps me to imitate God who is a worker and it brings out the usefulness and beauty of His earth. The purpose of my work is to love my neighbors as Jesus commands which brings me joy.
> - **Lie about my purpose: Work is a curse or a burden.** I should do the minimum amount of work because I get paid so little and my supervisors are not good people. My work is meaningless and always frustrating.

Imagination Exercise.

- **Directions.** Put yourself into the story. Imagine that you are Joseph or Josephina. Please close your eyes and imagine how this situation makes you feel. You work very hard to spread God's blessings to all of Potiphar's household, only to be falsely accused and thrown in prison. You were promoted to be a manager of his large house and farm, but now you are back on the bottom – even lower than before. Instead of living in Potiphar's beautiful house, you now are confined to a cramped, smelly, and dark dungeon.

- **Read from Genesis.** [With students' eyes still closed, read Genesis 39:20.]

- **Discuss.** "You may open your eyes now. While or as you imagined you were Joseph or Josephina being demoted from a trusted manager of a large household into a lowly prisoner for a crime you didn't commit, what feelings and thoughts are you tempted to dwell on? [Discuss.] You obviously need to hear from God to regain a godly perspective. Wouldn't it be great to get a letter from God in that moment? I'd like you to take a few moments now to write down what you think God would tell you to remind you of who you are and why you're here." Base it on things God has said in the Bible. [Give them 5-8 minutes to write their letters from God. Then have them break into pairs and read their letters to each other. Then ask who thinks their partner wrote something that the whole class should hear. Listen to 3-5 letters from girls as well as boys.]

Summary.

8. Why I'm Here: Good Work

- **Summary Statement.** Rather than being crushed by hard circumstances, remember your identity as God's child and your role as His representative. Drawing on this deep inner strength from God, you can do good work with God's help to make everything around you better for everyone.

- **Example of Jesus.** Even more than Joseph, Jesus stayed connected to God as the source of His good work. Jesus poured His whole heart into healing the sick, raising the dead, freeing people from evil spirits, and teaching about His Father's kingdom which is coming to earth as it is in heaven. When powerful people opposed this kingdom, Jesus continued His work of spreading His Father's blessings – even allowing His opponents to kill Him. What they thought was surely the end of Jesus was actually the beginning of multiplying co-workers in God's mission to bless the whole world.

- **Summary Scripture.** Here is a verse of scripture that is a good summary of how you can live out this lesson. Listen to Colossians 3:23-24: "In all the work you are doing, work the best you can. Work as if you were working for the Lord, not for men. Remember that you will receive your reward from the Lord, which he promised to his people. You are serving the Lord Christ."

- **Summary Questions.** [Instruct students to give a thumbs up/down sign or shout out yes/no.]

    (1) Do negative circumstance have to overwhelm us? *No*

    (2) Can we choose to let God rather than people tell us who we are? *Yes*

    (3) Is working with excellence a way we can imitate God? *Yes*

    (4) Does having a close relationship with God bless me only? *No*

    (5) When I am mistreated at work, should I do as little work as possible? *No*

    (6) Is work a good gift from God even though it is sometimes frustrating? *Yes*

    (7) Does God delight to share his work with his people? *Yes*

Assign Homework.

- **Option A.** Do something to bless others in a situation where you are not being treated fairly and see how it changes things.

- **Option B.** Do your very best in your schoolwork this week – asking God to work with you.

Closing Prayer. [If time is short, pray for the students. Otherwise, ask students to pray in pairs or small groups.]
Take out your letter from God and say a silent prayer in response to it – seeking God's help to live out this lesson.

9. Why I'm Here: Trusting God

Supplies – Blindfolds for each student.

FIRST HALF – 45 minutes

Review Previous Lesson's Homework. [Have each adult lead a small group of students in sharing how their homework went. Adults record who did their homework as credit toward graduation.]

Share the title of today's lesson and how it fits into the course as a whole. [Review with students the "Opportunity Makers Overview" from the Appendix to remind them of how today's lesson connects to what they have been learning. For example, remind them of the Identity Statement (for lessons 1-5) or Purpose Statement (for lessons 6-12) and the truths from previous lessons. If possible, show these things on the whiteboard as well.]

Opening Prayer. [Pray.]

Student Activity.

- **Explain.** [Break class into pairs and give each pair a blindfold] "We are going to do a trust walk. One in each pair will put on the blindfold then the one who can see will move five steps away and call the blind person's name over and over, guiding then around any obstacles. The blind person will follow that voice, walking until he/she joins hands with the seeing person. Then switch the blindfold to the other person and repeat the same exercise."

- **Do.** [Tell students to begin following the above instructions, while all of the adults help to monitor closely for safety. Help slow pairs to catch up with others so that exercise only takes two minutes per trust walk.]

- **Debrief.** Tell us about your experience of walking blind. [Discuss.]
  Were you confident in following the voice that was guiding you? Shout out yes or no. Each of you were somewhere between trust and fear. I want you to show me using your arms. If you were mostly trusting of your partner to guide you safely, put both of your arms out with your palms up.
  [Demonstrate with open outstretched hands.]
  If you were mostly fearful that following your partners voice would injure you, then put both hands on your head [demonstrate self-protecting posture]. If you were part trusting and part fearful, put one hand out and one

hand on your head. Keep your hands where they are while we talk about it. Why were you trusting or fearful or both?

[Call on two students from each of the three postures to share why they reacted as they did.]

Teach the Truth and Lie.

- **Transition.** Life is like walking blind. You cannot see your future, but you can choose to follow the voice of the one who lovingly guides you toward the good future He has for you.

- **Read the Truth and Lie.** Today's entire lesson is built upon this biblical truth. Please read it aloud with me [from whiteboard or poster on wall where students can be reminded of the topic throughout the lesson].

    - **Truth about my purpose: I can trust God** to work for my good as I focus on obeying His Word. Since my future is secure in God's hands, I can take bold risks to do good today, knowing that all will be well in the end.

    - **Lie about my purpose: I cannot trust God with my life and future.** He might ask me to do something difficult, and I am afraid I will lose what I already have or suffer the shame of failure. So, I submit to no one. I am my own provider. With no one looking out for me, I must take care of myself. No one else will.

- **Explain.** As you learned from walking blindfolded everything depends on how much you can trust the person who is guiding you. God is 100% worthy of your trust because He made you, is good, wants the best for you, and has the power to bring about the good future He has planned for you. Because of who God is, you can be confident in obeying His voice as He guides you through His Word and His Spirit. This doesn't mean you will not experience pain, but rather that He will be with you through it all, sharing your burdens and strengthening your character. Although you cannot always see it now, God is working everything out for your good in the end. He even brings good out of evil things that happen to you. So, you must take confident steps in the dark when God calls you to do something big to bless others. As you take care of God's work, He takes care of you. You can trust your good Father with your life and future.

    [Explain the truth further in your own words if necessary.]

- **Support with Scripture.** Listen to Proverbs 3:5-6: "Trust the Lord with all your heart. Don't depend on your own understanding. Remember the Lord in everything you do. And he will give you success." Notice that it says to trust "with all your heart," not half trusting [hold one hand out as in the blindfolded trust walk] and half fearful [other hand protecting your head]! Fear will paralyze you from obeying God's voice. It says: "Don't

9. Why I'm Here: Trusting God 77

depend on your own understanding." Remember that you are blind in a way – you don't know what's best for you and you can't see the future. But it's awesome that the only Person who does see the future has given His Word and His Spirit to guide you to a good future that is part of His plan to heal the whole world! Hallelujah!"

- **Illustrate.** Another picture of trusting our lives to God is being trapped in a tall burning building. Imagine that you cannot go down the stairs to escape because the lower floors are already filled with fire and smoke. The building is about to collapse, the heat and smoke is overwhelming, and the flames are coming at you. Thankfully, there is a window you can open to get some fresh air. You are high in the air and afraid of heights but as you look far below, you see that the firefighters are spreading a blanket to catch you if you can find the courage to jump. That is the leap of faith. It seems like a contradiction, but the safest thing you could do is to make a very scary jump out of a high window. In life, the alternative to trusting God is a disaster! Sinful and foolish apart from God, trying to control your own life is like setting it on fire. Trying to take care of yourself will ruin your life and prevent you from experiencing exciting adventures of joining God in His mission. So jump into the arms of your good Father.

Example of Joseph.

- **Transition.** Joseph certainly threw himself into the arms of God each time his life was on fire. Every time it looked like God had abandoned him, he chose to believe that God was still good rather than depending on his own understanding. He resisted the flood of fear and despair for 13 long years of hard times.

- **Read from Genesis.** [Read Genesis 37:18-28.] That passage tells us what was happening to Joseph on the outside. Now let's listen to what was happening inside Joseph's heart and how that made all the difference in his life. [Read Genesis 49:22-27]

- **Discuss.** How did Joseph keep from being consumed with anger toward his brothers? [Discuss.]

    [Hints…]
    - Even though he was alone when his brothers rejected him, he trusted that God was with him.
    - He knew that the God who kept his promises to his Father was still in control and could bring good out of evil as he said to his brother much later: "You meant to hurt me. But God turned your evil into good. It was to save the lives of many people." [Genesis 50:20]

Listen again to how God helped Joseph in his troubles. [Read Genesis 49:22-24.]

What actions could help you turn to God and lean on His strength when you face trials?

[Hints…]

- Pray | read your bible | memorize God's promises | go to church
- ask for prayer and encouragement from Christian family, leaders and friends.

Closing Prayer. [Thank God for key biblical insights uncovered during the lesson.]

9. Why I'm Here: Trusting God

SECOND HALF – 45 minutes

Opening Prayer. [Pray.]

Re-read Truth and Lie.

> - **Truth about my purpose: I can trust God** to work for my good as I focus on obeying His Word. Since my future is secure in God's hands, I can take bold risks to do good today, knowing that all will be well in the end.
>
> - **Lie about my purpose: I cannot trust God with my life and future.** He might ask me to do something difficult, and I am afraid I will lose what I already have or suffer the shame of failure. So, I submit to no one. I am my own provider. With no one looking out for me, I must take care of myself. No one else will.

Imagination Exercise.

- **Directions.** Put yourself into the story. Imagine that you are Joseph and your brother have just thrown you into a deep well. With no water in it, you fell and hurt yourself when hitting the hard bottom, possible breaking a rib and you're sore all over. It's dark and cold and you feel so alone. You're not sure whether you're hurting more physically or emotionally. You wonder if you will die of thirst, and you feel so helpless. You miss your dad who is so far way and your mom who died years ago. You are tempted to give into the wolves of fear and despair that lunge at your heart.

    If you could see the future when you would be working with the king to feed the whole country during a seven-year food shortage, what one sentence would you repeat to yourself over and over to beat back fear and despair?

    Write that sentence down.

- **Read from Genesis.** Pretend you are Joseph as we read that part of his story.
[Read Genesis 37:18-24. Repeat the *italicized* question and ask students to write down their answer during two minutes of silence.]

- **Discuss.** Turn to someone beside you and listen to their sentence of encouragement. [Give them a minute to share in pairs.]
Now, whose partner wrote a message that all of us should hear? [Have a few of the nominated students read their sentences.]

Summary.

- **Summary Statement.** Although you are blind to the future, God is *not* and can be your trustworthy guide to the good future He leads you toward. God is worthy of your trust because He is both good and powerful. So, trust Him with your life and future, knowing that He suffers with you in your trials and will bring good out of them. Even though trusting Him can be scary, God knows best. Lean on Him for strength and as you do His will even when it is challenging.

- **Example of Jesus.** Trusting God does not mean we won't be tempted to avoid suffering. Even Jesus was not happy about the agony of the cross He knew was coming. Luke 22:44 says

    "Jesus was full of pain; he prayed even more. Sweat dripped from his face as if he was bleeding."

    Just like Joseph, Jesus trusted that God would bring much good out of the evil He would suffer: "He kneeled down and prayed:

    "Father, if it is what you want, then let me not have this cup of suffering. But do what you want, not what I want."

    He submitted to God's will and obeyed, believing that His good Father would bring a good result in the end. It was actually the best result *ever* since Christ's suffering restored all those who believe to a right relationship with God. It also led to Christ's resurrection which guaranteed that the whole world – including our own bodies – will be restored.

- **Summary Scripture.** Let's listen to a verse that was true in the lives of Joseph and Jesus. It will be true of yours too as you trust in God...Romans 8:28:

    "We know that in everything God works for the good of those who love him. They are the people God called, because that was his plan."

- **Summary Questions.** [Instruct students to give a thumbs up/down sign or shout out yes/no.]
    (1) Does trusting God guarantee that nothing bad will happen to us? *No*
    (2) Does God promise to be with us and help bear our trials? *Yes*
    (3) Does God bring good out of the evil that happens to His people? *Yes*
    (4) Does trusting God mean we will never struggle with fear or despair? *No*
    (5) Is God in control of the future and committed to do us good? *Yes*
    (6) Is it okay for me to make my own decisions and ignore God's will? *No*
    (7) Will obeying God always make sense according to human wisdom? *No*

9. Why I'm Here: Trusting God

Assign Homework.

- **Option A.** What cause you to fear or lose hope? Write a prayer of trust about that situation and use it when you need it.
- **Option B.** Find the sentence of encouragement you wrote when imagining you were thrown into an empty well. Write this sentence in a place where you'll see it all this week. The go read and reflect on it whenever you are tempted to doubt that God is with you and has a good plan for you.

Closing Prayer. [If time is short, pray for the students. Otherwise, ask students to pray in pairs or small groups.]

Psalm 23 is a prayer of trust in a good God who is with us in our trials, so let's pray this version of it out loud together:

"You Lord are my shepherd. I have everything I need.

You give me rest in green pastures. You lead me to calm water.

You give me new strength. For the good of your name, you lead me on paths that are right.

Even if I walk through a very dark valley, I will not be afraid because you are with me. Your rod and your shepherd's staff comfort me.

You prepare a meal for me in front of my enemies. You pour oil of blessing on my head. You give me more than I can hold.

Surely your goodness and love will be with me all my life. And I will live in the house of the Lord forever."

10. Why I'm Here: Shaping the Future

Supplies. Colored markers or Crayons for each student.

FIRST HALF – 45 minutes

Review Previous Lesson's Homework. [Have each adult lead a small group of students in sharing how their homework went. Adults record who did their homework as credit toward graduation.]

Share the title of today's lesson and how it fits into the course as a whole. [Review with students the "Opportunity Makers Overview" from the Appendix to remind them of how today's lesson connects to what they have been learning. For example, remind them of the Identity Statement (for lessons 1-5) or Purpose Statement (for lessons 6-12) and the truths from previous lessons. If possible, show these things on the whiteboard as well.]

Opening Prayer. [Pray.]

Student Activity.

- **Explain** – I want you to think of a big problem in your community that you wish God would instantly solve. What name would you give to that problem? In one or two words write the name of your problem really large on a piece of paper.

- **Do** - [Give each student a piece of paper and colored markers. Give them two minutes to draw the title to fill the entire page.]

- **Debrief** - Please hold up your papers so everyone can see them. [Ask a student to rapidly read all the titles of the community problems to the class.] Do you have any hope that your community problem will ever be solved? Put your thumbs up for yes or thumbs down for no. If so, how many years do you think it will take to fix it? [Discuss.] Did you ever think that God may want to work with *you* to solve this community problem - even if takes a long time to see any progress? A group of Christians including politician William Wilberforce and author Hannah More worked hard to oppose the British slave trade, but for many years it looked hopeless because so many powerful people in England were making lots of money by buying and selling Africans into slavery. Every year Wilberforce introduced a proposed law to the Parliament [government leaders] and every year it was defeated. But they persevered for 20 long years. It finally passed in 1807. That was a long time to keep doing the right thing even though it looked hopeless. Like with Joseph, God finally made things right after many years of difficult human effort and leaning on God.

Teach the Truth and Lie.

- **Transition.** Like William Wilberforce and Hanna More, God wants to work through you to shape the future of your community.

- **Read the Truth and Lie.** Today's entire lesson is built upon this biblical truth. Please read it aloud with me [from whiteboard or poster on wall where students can be reminded of the topic throughout the lesson].

    > **Truth about my purpose: My actions can really shape the future** for me and my community. I am called to make my community better by my godly character and actions. God empowers me to make good things happen as I depend on Him. I can join with others to create new opportunities. Our God-given creativity can conceive them, and our determination can achieve them.

    > **Lie about my purpose: I am a victim.** My negative circumstances define me. Bad people and experiences entrap me. I have no ability to change the future. I must accept my fate. I am trapped in poverty. I have no hope that things will get better. Surviving is my only goal. Dreams of the future are a luxury I cannot afford. I don't have enough money, education, strength, or connections to pursue dreams that will never come true.

- **Explain.** What you believe will powerfully shape your future. Imagine two girls who both have the same difficult life circumstances - no opportunity to go to school because one parent has left, and the other has no work. If one girl has a positive outlook and hope for the future, she will have a much different life than the girl who gives up and accepts her fate as a poor victim who cannot dream for a better future. Do you believe this? [Discuss.] You can either crumple inward or cheerfully make life better for everyone around you. Ironically, as we see in the life of Joseph, those who work hard to build a better future for *others* find that they themselves are rewarded in the process. [Explain the truth further in your own words if necessary.]

- **Support with Scripture.** "Let's listen to Colossians 1:29:

    "To do this, I work and struggle, using Christ's great strength that works so powerfully in me.'

    This scripture shows us that God empowers our work to accomplish His plans. And what are God's plans? He's creating a bright, good future as we see in our next verse, Jeremiah 29:11:

10. Why I'm Here: Shaping the Future

> "I say this because I know what I have planned for you,' says the Lord. 'I have good plans for you. I don't plan to hurt you. I plan to give you hope and a good future.' So, as we depend on Him, God uses our actions to shape a better future for us and our communities."

- **Illustrate.** A good example is God's design for business. It takes a hugely positive view of the future to start a business. When you create solutions for others by providing needed products and services, it creates wealth for both you and the people you are able to hire. So surprisingly, focusing outward is the best way to improve your own future - just like Joseph.

Example of Joseph.

- **Transition.** Joseph certainly had hope in the most hopeless of circumstances: slavery and prison. Even in those places, he worked hard to serve others which made his life better in both the present and the future. What gave him this positive attitude that led him to take initiative that shape the future? The answer: he knew *who* he was and *why* he was here. He had unshakable confidence in every aspect of the God-given identity and purpose we've discussed in this course. Think of each of these as essential nutrients for a soul to be healthy:

  [Write these as bullet points on a whiteboard.]

  - Being defined by God alone.
  - Believing he was a cherished child of God.
  - Realizing that God seeks to restore harmony to broken relationships.
  - Believing that God could bless and shape him through hardship.
  - Realizing that his life needed to reflect God to the world.
  - Trusting that God had a good plan for his life.
  - Knowing he was responsible for developing God's gifts to him.
  - Seeing that work was a good way to partner with God to make life better for everyone around him.
  - And being confident that he could trust God to do him good.

  When thrown into prison for a crime he didn't commit, the above soul nutrients steered him away from depression and suicide and toward how his prison experience actually went, which we'll read now.

- **Read from Genesis.** [Read Genesis 41:33-40. Under the above essential soul nutrients on the whiteboard write "depression and suicide" on the left and "excelling in service to others" on the right, drawing a vertical line in between them.]

If you were imprisoned for several years for a crime you didn't commit, would your life be closer to the left or to the right? [Discuss.]

How deeply have these "essential soul nutrients" become part of who you are? [Discuss.]

The way he lived as a slave and prisoner shaped his future and the future of the whole country. Listen now to Joseph's wise advice right after he shared God's interpretation of the king's dream about the coming seven-year food shortage. [Read Genesis 41:33-40.]

Does this sound like the average slave or prisoner?

What prepared him to think like that in the moment and give such wise advice about the future?

- **Discuss.** [Hints…]
    - He did his work so well and asked for more.
    - He took initiative to add to his responsibilities, then followed through with excellence.
    - As he earned more trust, he was given more authority and learned how to use it well. This developed his God-given gifts as a leader who looks ahead and sees a better future for everyone.

[Draw the following diagram on a whiteboard.]

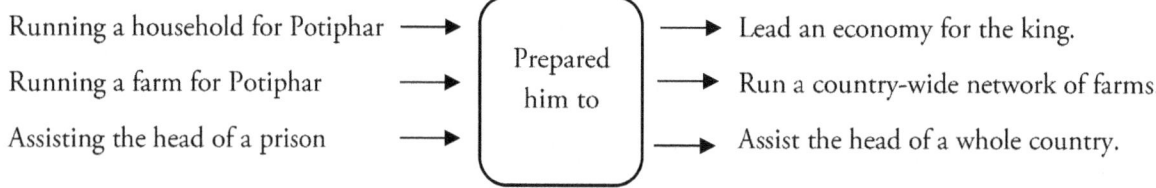

Seeking and taking opportunities right in front of him prepared him for larger opportunities that would come later. Instead of just letting the future happen, what does Joseph advise the king to do? [Discuss.]

[Hints…]
- He suggested that the king look ahead and make plans to shape the future, including appointing leaders, gathering one fifth of all the food that is produced, storing it in each city, guarding the stored food from thieves, then distributing it during the food shortage. We too must make prayerful plans for the future good of our communities.

Closing Prayer. [Thank God for key biblical insights uncovered during the lesson.]

10. Why I'm Here: Shaping the Future

SECOND HALF – 45 minutes

Opening Prayer. [Pray.]

Re-read Truth and Lie.

> - **Truth about my purpose: My actions can really shape the future** for me and my community. I am called to make my community better by my godly character and actions. God empowers me to make good things happen as I depend on Him. I can join with others to create new opportunities. Our God-given creativity can conceive them, and our determination can achieve them.
> - **Lie about my purpose: I am a victim.** My negative circumstances define me. Bad people and experiences entrap me. I have no ability to change the future. I must accept my fate. I am trapped in poverty. I have no hope that things will get better. Surviving is my only goal. Dreams of the future are a luxury I cannot afford. I don't have enough money, education, strength, or connections to pursue dreams that will never come true.

Imagination Exercise.

- **Directions.** "Put yourself into the story. Choose quickly whether you will be Potiphar, the prison warden, or one of Joseph's family members. Raise your hand to tell me who you decided to be: Potiphar…prison warden…family member. It is now 14 years after Genesis 41 passage we read where Joseph proposed a 14-year plan to prepare for and endure a disastrous food shortage. Everything turned out well and now I am a news reporter writing a book about Joseph's life. I am looking for clues to his success from early in his life. I want to interview you to see what insight you can give me for my book. I'll give you a few minutes to think about my question and write down some notes before the interview in front of this audience. My question is: 'What about Joseph's past made him so good at shaping the future?'"
[Write the question on a whiteboard and give students 3-5 minutes to write their answer.]

- **Discuss.** "I hear that some of Joseph's family members are here today as well as those who supervised him when he was a slave and a prisoner. 'Who has some insight into this question I need to answer in my book?'"
[Discuss their answers to: "What about Joseph's past made him so good at shaping the future?"]

Summary.

- **Summary Statement.** God wants to work through you to shape the future of your community. You can't do this without being hopeful about the future. This hope comes from deeply believing what God says about who you are and why you're here. These essential soul nutrients give you a positive attitude that enables you to tackle today's small opportunities with excellence in preparation for bigger opportunities later. Instead of being devastated by trials, you can excel in serving others. As you take responsibility to solve their problems, your abilities grow, and you gain more influence to shape a better future for both you and your community.

- **Example of Jesus.** Like Joseph, Jesus worked with the Father to secure a better future for others. Joseph's planning saved from starvation God's people into which Jesus was eventually born. And the sacrificial work of Jesus has reconciled generations of people to God - including us. There are more parts to God's plan for saving our future with hm than we have time to discuss today, so let's focus on one small slice - Jesus intentionally invested in training 12 disciples over a three-year period. He lived and ate with them, taught them and prayed with them, and invited them into his work. Before ascending to heaven, he said in Acts 1:8:

  > "But the Holy Spirit will come to you. Then you will receive power. You will be my witness - in Jerusalem, in all of Judea, in Samaria, and in every part of the world."

  So he left them with a plan to bring all he had imparted to them to the whole world and gave them the Holy Spirit's power to do so. They are to speak and live out the truth that Jesus is king. The ways we are called to build the future are part of this big plan of God for His world.

- **Summary Scripture.** Let's listen to 1 Corinthians 3:9-11:

  > "We are workers together for God. And you are like a farm that belongs to God. And you are a house that belongs to God. Like an expert builder I built the foundation of that house. I used the gift that God gave me to do this. Others are building on that foundation. But everyone should be careful how he builds. The foundation has already been built. No one can build any other foundation. The foundation that has already been laid is Jesus Christ."

  It is a remarkable privilege that we can work alongside God Almighty to build the future He has in mind.

- **Summary Questions.** [Instruct students to give a thumbs up/down sign or shout out yes/no.]

  (1) Should I give up on life and accept my fate as a poor victim when trials come? *No*

  (2) Will what I believe about who I am and why I am here shape my future? *Yes*

  (3) Does focusing my life on serving others actually improve my own future too? *Yes*

  (4) Will doing well with small responsibilities today prepare me for bigger opportunities later? *Yes*

  (5) Should I just let the future happen instead of taking initiative to shape it? *No*

  (6) Should I pray and plan for a better future for me and my community? *Yes*

Assign Homework.

- Option A. Look again at the big community problem you wrote down at the beginning of this lesson. Thinking like Joseph who made a 14-year plan to overcome a massive food shortage, write down all the steps you can think of toward solving that problem. Then pick one of those steps and see if you and people you know can start working on it prayerfully.
- Option B. Look at the list of "essential soul nutrients" that we've been learning about in this course. Which two are the most true of you and which two do you most hope to grow in? Share those four answers with a leader you trust at home or at church. Ask her or him to pray for you and help you grow.

Closing Prayer. [Ask students to pray in pairs or small groups if there's time. Then close by having each student lift up their page which names the community problem they want God to solve. Ask them to lift those problems up to God in prayer silently. Then pray a prayer of blessing over them, including asking God to use them as a part of how He answers their prayers for their community.]

11. Why I'm Here: Teamwork

FIRST HALF – 45 minutes

Review Previous Lesson's Homework. [Have each adult lead a small group of students in sharing how their homework went. Adults record who did their homework as credit toward graduation.]

Share the title of today's lesson and how it fits into the course as a whole. [Review with students the "Opportunity Makers Overview" from the Appendix to remind them of how today's lesson connects to what they have been learning. For example, remind them of the Identity Statement (for lessons 1-5) or Purpose Statement (for lessons 6-12) and the truths from previous lessons. If possible, show these things on the whiteboard as well.]

Opening Prayer. [Pray.]

Student Activity.

- **Explain.** [Break class into trios.] I would like each group to answer the following question and write down three reasons to support your answer.
  Is it better to make and eat cake by yourself or with a group?

- **Do.** [Write the question on a whiteboard and monitor groups to keep them on track and make sure they understand the exercise and are writing down reasons why they feel their answer is correct.]

- **Debrief.** Let's have a spokesperson from each group share your answer and your supporting reasons with the class [Discuss.]
  Life is like cake. How you see cake reveals a mindset of scarcity or abundance. You can either think that a larger piece for her means a smaller piece for you or realize that together you can make a bigger and better cake. This gives you more to enjoy and even share with others. Plus, you will likely enjoy your cake more when you eat it together with friends!

Teach the Truth and Lie.

- **Transition.** God has made us to live together in mutually beneficial relationships.

- **Read the Truth and Lie.** Today's entire lesson is built upon this biblical truth. Please read it aloud with me [from whiteboard or poster on wall where students can be reminded of the topic throughout the lesson].

  ➢ **Truth about my purpose: I cannot fulfill God's purpose alone**, so I must build strong teamwork. We can solve bigger problems together as we rely on other's encouragement, ideas, and God-given abilities.

Because God made us for joyful fellowship, our strengths don't merely *add* together. They *multiply* when we work together. Even when my teammates do wrong, God can still bring good from it. So, I must work together with others to create good solutions for our community.

> **Lie about my purpose: I cannot trust anyone.** I do not need others since I can do things by myself. People only hurt me so I should rely on myself alone.

- **Explain.** [Explain the truth further in your own words if necessary.] When we work together, the results are almost always better than when everyone works alone. Why do you think that is true? [Discuss.]

    [Hints…]
    - Everyone brings different gifts and perspectives that improve the solution.
    - Having teammates encourages each person when the work is hard.
    - Teamwork pushes each person to do their best.
    - Teams provide accountability to finish the job.

    And when we work together, we can tackle bigger problems than we could on our own. This is important if we're going to truly shape a better future for our communities - as we discussed in the previous lesson. Plus, when we work together, each person can focus on using their strongest gifts from God instead of trying to do everything by themselves. This extra time using their gifts makes those abilities even stronger. So, when you bring people together in teamwork, you are helping to develop God's gifts in others as well as in yourself. This helps each team member to appreciate each other more as you see each other's gifts really shine. When you solve a problem together, you have more people to celebrate your good work with!

- **Support with Scripture.** Here is a passage of Scripture that paints the perfect picture of what we're saying. Teamwork benefits both the work results and the relationships developed through it. Let's listen to Ecclesiastes 4:9-12:

    "Two people are better than one.

    They get more done by working together.

    If one person falls, the other can help him up.

    But it is bad for the person who is alone when he falls.

    No one is there to help him.

    If two lie down together, they will be warm.

    But a person alone will not be warm.

11. Why I'm Here: Teamwork

> An enemy might defeat one person,
>
> > but two people together can defend themselves.
>
> A rope that has three parts wrapped together
>
> > is hard to break."

- **Illustrate.** Teamwork is like the tide that raises all boats. Each person is a single boat. A lack of teamwork is like shallow water wherein the boats are getting stuck in the mud and can't fulfill their purposes. But when the water of teamwork is added, then each boat can fulfill its purpose: fishing boats can fish, sailboats can sail, speed boats can speed, and tugboats can tug.

Example of Joseph.

- **Transition.** Teamwork multiplies what team members already have within themselves – for good or evil. Look at Joseph's brothers – as a group they become bolder in their plans to hurt Joseph. Let's listen in….

- **Read from Genesis.** [Read Genesis 37:18-20, 26-28, 31-32.]

- **Discuss.** By themselves, it is doubtful that any one of Joseph's brothers would have sold him into slavery and lied to their father that he was dead. Family is a God-given team, but Joseph's brothers rebelled against God's purpose to use that teamwork for good. Even though some people will fail you, God is able to turn those painful disappointments into something good and beautiful in the end. As we're about to read, Joseph forgave them and restored the encouragement and generosity that God intended for a family team.

    [Read Genesis 50:20-21.] "Strength in numbers" can be used for either evil or good and Joseph certainly had a huge assignment that he could not do alone.

    [Read Genesis 41:33-36.] Joseph will need a strong team in each city to carry out his 14-year plan successfully. What roles should be appointed on each team?

    [Hints:]

    team leader | collection agent | storage manager | security guard | distribution manager.

Closing Prayer. [Thank God for key biblical insights uncovered during the lesson.]

SECOND HALF – 45 minutes

Opening Prayer.

Re-read Truth and Lie.

> ➢ **Truth about my purpose: I cannot fulfill God's purpose alone**, so I must build strong teamwork. We can solve bigger problems together as we rely on other's encouragement, ideas, and God-given abilities. Because God made us for joyful fellowship, our strengths don't merely *add* together. They *multiply* when we work together. Even when my teammates do wrong, God can still bring good from it. So, I must work together with others to create good solutions for our community.
>
> ➢ **Lie about my purpose: I cannot trust anyone.** I do not need others since I can do things by myself. People only hurt me so I should rely on myself alone.

Imagination Exercise.

- **Directions.** Put yourself into the story. We are one of Joseph's leadership teams assigned to anticipate and fix problems in this 14-year food shortage and distribution program in your own city. What are some problems that could arrive? [Discuss.]

    [Hints...]

    - Thieves
    - Flooding
    - Insects
    - Mold
    - Not saving enough
    - People taking more than they need
    - Not having enough storage barns
    - (Ideas from the class)

[Break into trios and give each "city team" one problem to solve from the above list. Pass out the problems on slips of paper you prepared in advance so each group can begin quickly rather than waiting for you to talk to each group separately. Atop the page that identifies their problem, put one of these city names from ancient Egypt: Memphis, Thebes, Alexandria, Amarna, Abydos, Hermopolis, Crocodilopolis, Elephantine, and Kom Ombo. Ask them to choose a spokesperson to take notes to share with the whole class. Give them 5-7 minutes to discuss their solutions to the following two questions you write on a whiteboard.]

How would you try to prevent this problem?

If it happened anyway, how would you stop it?

11. Why I'm Here: Teamwork

- **Discuss.** Let's re-gather to hear your solutions. [Discuss briefly – giving each group only one minute.]

  Tell me about a moment during your city team discussion when a team member built on another team member's idea which led to a better solution. [Discuss.]

  How much better was your team's solution than if only one of you had tried to solve it alone?

Summary

- **Summary Statement.** You can solve bigger problems together as you rely on other's encouragement, ideas, and God-given abilities. Because God made you for joyful fellowship, your strengths don't merely *add* together. They *multiply* when you work together. Even when teammates or whole teams do the wrong things, God can still bring good from it. So, work together with others to create good solutions for your community.

- **Example of Jesus.** Even though He is God in flesh, Jesus still involved teams in his work, including his 12 disciples whom he called "brothers", a group of women who provided financial support, and 72 disciples that He sent out to spread the good news of God's Kingdom. When He fed the multitudes, He started with five loaves of bread and two fish that the people already had. After praying over the food, He invited His disciples to be part of the miracle of seeing the food multiply as they distributed it. When He gave them jobs to do together, it strengthened the teamwork they would lean on for years to come as they spread the good news and built the church.

- **Summary Scripture.** Listen to 1 Corinthians 12:19-21, 27:

  > "If each part of the body were the same part, there would be no body. But truly God put the parts in the body as he wanted them. He made a place for each one of them. And so there are many parts, but only one body. The eye cannot say to the hand, 'I don't need you!' And the head cannot say to the foot, 'I don't need you!' All of you together are the body of Christ. Each one of you is a part of that body."

  We need each other!

- **Summary Questions.** [Instruct students to give a thumbs up/down sign or shout out yes/no.]

  (1) Can we produce the best solutions all by ourselves? *No*

  (2) When teammates hurt me, should I withdraw from others? *No*

  (3) Is God able to bring good out of broken teamwork? *Yes*

  (4) Can we solve even bigger problems for our communities when we work together? *Yes*

  (5) Does teamwork follow God's intention for his people? *Yes*

(6) Do I have all of the needed gifts in myself alone? *No*

(7) Does good teamwork multiply the strengths of team members? *Yes*

Assign Homework.

- **Option A.** What is something that you can accomplish with someone's help that you can't do alone? Ask for help from someone. As you work together, notice how their gifts are different from yours and discuss your teamwork with him/her.

- **Option B.** Recall a time when a teammate hurt you. Give that wound to God in prayer and ask God to show you something good that he brought out of your pain.

Closing Prayer. [If time is short, pray for the students. Otherwise, ask students to pray in pairs or small groups.] Have students pray in pairs to apply this lesson in their lives, then pray Romans 15:5-6 over them...]

> "Patience and encouragement come from God. And I pray that God will help you all agree with each other the way Christ Jesus wants. Then you will all be joined together, and you will give glory to God the Father of our Lord Jesus Christ."

12. Why I'm Here: Generosity

Supplies. See student activity for details about the following supplies: colored paper and nametags.

FIRST HALF – 45 minutes

Review Previous Lesson's Homework. [Have each adult lead a small group of students in sharing how their homework went. Adults record who did their homework as credit toward graduation.]

Share the title of today's lesson and how it fits into the course as a whole. [Review with students the "Opportunity Makers Overview" from the Appendix to remind them of how today's lesson connects to what they have been learning. For example, remind them of the Identity Statement (for lessons 1-5) or Purpose Statement (for lessons 6-12) and the truths from previous lessons. If possible, show these things on the whiteboard as well.]

Opening Prayer.

Student Activity.

- **Explain.** [Give half the students name tags that say "Generous" and the other half nametags that say "Greedy." Write the following instructions on the whiteboard…]

  <u>Generous: give as much as you can.</u> | <u>Greedy: Get as much as you can.</u>

  [Make a large number of small slips of colored paper to represent money – about 20 slips per student. Give 10 slips to each student and the rest to an adult with "Employer" on their nametag. Three other adults should wear these name tags: church, school, and natural disaster response. Have each adult sit at a table with a container for money slips and lots of paper & pencil or pens.

    - At the employer table, students can earn one slip by drawing a tool that can be used at work such as: an axe, ladder | computer | desk | hammer | sewing machine | telephone | saw | drill | shovel | rake | hoe | broom | hair dryer | hairbrush | scissors | paint brush | taxi | bus | book.

    - At the church, school, and natural disaster response tables, students can either donate "money" slips or time.

    - To volunteer their time, they must draw the following:
        - ✓ At church: flowers they will deliver to the elderly with a hug.
        - ✓ At natural disaster relief: food | clothes | tents.

✓ At school: animals for a wall mural (octopus, elephant, kangaroo, zebra, giraffe, camel, ostrich, crocodile, etc.) they are painting to make the children happy.]

Okay, my "Generous" and "Greedy" friends, I will now give you 10 minutes to go to these four tables and figure out how to follow the instructions I wrote on the whiteboard. You can earn more "money" slips at the employer table and the other three tables have opportunities to donate both your money and your time to make other people smile.

- **Do.** Go! [Monitor the students and clarify the instructions as needed during the 10-minute exercise.]

- **Debrief.**
  a. Who had more fun – the "Generous" or the "Greedy"? [Discuss.]
  b. Who feels more joyful and why? [Discuss.]

  [Hint…]

  - We are joyful when giving because we are reflecting God as we were designed to do.
  - Why does a bird love to fly? Because that's what it's made for!

  c. Who inspired more joy and gratitude at the church, school, and natural disaster response? [Discuss.]
  d. Who built more good relationships with people who would help you when you need it? [Discuss.
  e. Who is richer? [Discuss.]

  [Hint…] Relationships are a form of wealth.

  f. What can we learn from this exercise? [Discuss.]

  [Hints…]

  - Having strong relationships is a valuable and lasting type of wealth.
  - Work is more fulfilling when you do it for others.
  - There are several ways to be generous – with your money, time, creativity, and work.
  - When you give, you receive even more back.

Teach the Truth and Lie.

- **Transition.** You really *can* live a life of constant, joyful generosity.

- **Read the Truth and Lie.** Today's entire lesson is built upon this biblical truth. Please read it aloud with me [from whiteboard or poster on wall where students can be reminded of the topic throughout the lesson].

  ➢ **Truth about my purpose: I should constantly share what God has given me.** This is a reflection of God whose grace is always overflowing. God provides for me, so when I share with others, I don't have less. God will continue to bless me so that I can be even more generous. This multiplies joy as generosity strengthens our relationships. We are all grateful to God for His many good gifts.

> **Lie about my purpose: I am crippled by fear of what others will think or do.** Why should I create wealth that others will steal? Why should I share wealth and make myself vulnerable? I must keep my fists closed so I don't lose anything I have worked for.

- **Explain.** [Explain the truth further in your own words if necessary.]

We end this section on identity and purpose with generosity because by now we hope you realize how much you have to give – you are rich! A quick review of the riches we've discussed:

Who you are – defined by God's love, a cherished child, given relationships that God can heal, blessed even in suffering, and reflecting God to the world.

Why you're here – to live out God's good plan, develop God's gifts to you, do good work, trust in a good God, and shape the future with him and with others.

With all of this wealth, it makes sense that the final part of your purpose is to share it all with a broken world. You are blessed to be a blessing. As Jesus told us in (Acts 20:35), it truly "more blessed to give than to receive." When you give, both the giver and receiver are filled with joy and their relationship grows strong and becomes a bigger delight than the gift itself.

- **Support with Scripture.** These ideas come straight from the Bible. King Solomon shared this wisdom 3,000 years ago. Let's listen to Proverbs 11:24-25:

    "Some people give much but get back even more. But others don't give what they should, and they end up poor. A person who gives to others will get richer. Whoever helps others will himself be helped."

- **Illustrate.** I've heard the same thing over and over on mission trips and disaster relief trips. Volunteers, including students, almost always say: "I thought I was the one giving, but I ended up receiving more than I gave." Please raise your hand if you've ever felt that way. What are some of the things that those volunteers gained? [Discuss.]

    [Hints…]
    - Learning | growing | joy | gratitude | friendship | intimacy with God by joining Him in His work.

Example of Joseph.

- **Transition.** Joseph was definitely a strong example of the abundant generosity we're recommending to you. Thinking back to the life of Joseph, who are some of the people he was generous with and how? [Discuss.]

[Hints…]

- Potiphar and prison warden: Joseph gave extra effort far beyond what was asked of him.
- Cup bearer and king: Joseph offered God's interpretation of their dreams freely. He could have asked for money, freedom from prison, or some other reward.
- Whole country of Egypt: Joseph freely offered his wise advice in how to prepare for the food shortage, then used his gifts of leadership to coordinate the nationwide efforts to store then distribute the food.
- His family: Although Joseph helped his family survive the 7-year food shortage, the more remarkable generosity was the forgiveness he offered to the brothers who had thrown him in a pit, sold him into slavery and told his father Jacob that he was dead. Listen to what happened right after their father Jacob died.

- **Read from Genesis.** [Read Genesis 50:15-21.]

- **Discuss.** Joseph just kept giving: to Potiphar, the prison warden, the cup bearer, the king, the whole country of Egypt, and his own family. How did all this generosity bring blessings back to Joseph himself? [Discuss.]

    [Hints…]

    - Potiphar and the prison warden rewarded him with their trust, more responsibility, authority, and a measure of freedom that comes with being in charge.
    - After forgetting Joseph in prison for two years, the cup bearer finally remembered him when another dream needed interpreting: the king's.
    - Being generous with God's wisdom to the king led to Joseph's amazing rise from the prison to the palace. His position overseeing the storage and distribution of food led him to be reunited with his family while saving them from starvation. Working with God and others to save millions of lives was certainly rewarding as well!

It is easy to be generous when you have a lot and all is going well, but remember that Joseph's generosity that saved Egypt from starvation he also steadily practiced during 13 years of slavery and imprisonment! Although it took 13 long years of patient generosity while suffering as a slave and a prisoner, God did reward his generosity in amazing ways. So again, we see the truth that givers receive back much more than they give.

The idea of generosity strengthening relationships is shown to be true in Joseph's life as well. Saving your family and a whole country from starvation will certainly stir up some love and gratitude! A final lesson we can learn from Joseph's generosity is this: he credited God as being the ultimate source – the true Giver. He told the king [Genesis 41:16, 25]:

> "I am not able to explain the meaning of dreams. God will do this for the king…God is telling you what he is about to do"

Being humble in our giving encourages people to give thanks to God, the provider of all good things.

Closing Prayer. [Thank God for key biblical insights uncovered during the lesson.]

Opportunity Makers

SECOND HALF – 45 minutes

Opening Prayer.

Re-read Truth and Lie.

- > **Truth about my purpose: I should constantly share what God has given me.** This is a reflection of God whose grace is always overflowing. God provides for me, so when I share with others, I don't have less. God will continue to bless me so that I can be even more generous. This multiplies joy as generosity strengthens our relationships. We are all grateful to God for His many good gifts.
- > **Lie about my purpose: I am crippled by fear of what others will think or do.** Why should I create wealth that others will steal? Why should I share wealth and make myself vulnerable? I must keep my fists closed so I don't lose anything I have worked for.

Imagination Exercise.

- **Read from Genesis.** What happened when the cupbearer told Joseph his dream in prison?
  [Joseph interpreted his dream, then made the following request. Read Genesis 40.14.]
  Did the cupbearer do what he asked? *No*
  But what happened two years later? The king had a dream after which the cupbearer said the following.
  [Read Genesis 41.9-13.]

- **Directions.** Put yourself into the story. You are a group of historians writing down the history of the seven-year food shortage in Egypt but you're writing an alternative history – how it would have been if this one small thing had been different: instead of telling the cupbearer what his dream meant, a prisoner named Joseph was a stingy man who refused to help the cupbearer know the meaning of his dream.
  [Break into trios with an adult facilitating each one. Assign one of the three questions to each group for them to discuss for three minutes then report back to the whole class. Ask them to choose a spokesperson for their group. Write these three questions on the whiteboard:]
  1. What would have been different for Joseph?
  2. What would have been different for Egypt?
  3. What would have been different for Joseph's family?

- **Discuss.** Let's hear the spokesperson from each group tell the class how you have answered your question about the alternative history of Egypt's seven-year food shortage.

12. Why I'm Here: Generosity

Summary.

- **Summary Statement.** Being given a rich identity and purpose from God, you are blessed to be a constant blessing. As a conduit of God's grace, He keeps filling you up as you work with Him to pour into others. As you see in Joseph's life, working at your job is an important way you can bless others – through both the work itself and the money you earn. Giving doesn't make you poorer. It actually enriches you as you become "rich in good deeds" [1 Timothy 6:18] and receive the "life that is truly life" [1 Timothy 6:19].

  One form of wealth that generosity brings you is stronger relationships with those you give to. And you help them develop a closer relationship with God when your giving causes them to give thanks to the Lord. This is especially true when you point to God as the true source, which also reminds you that you are *not* God, but rather his co-worker. Generosity is a clear way to mirror this God whose grace overflows continuously like a fountain and like the life-giving rays of the sun.

- **Example of Jesus.** The life of Jesus was a constant flow of life-giving generosity culminating in giving His very life so that we can live eternally with His father. His constant giving included spending time with children, honoring women in a culture that did not, feeding the multitudes, turning water into very good wine, washing His disciples' feet and living daily with them, forgiving sins, freeing people from demons and diseases, raising the lame to their feet and the dead back to life. He shared good news and He *is* good news: His *life* showed us what God is like. His *death* freed us from our sin. His *resurrection* guarantees our own. Jesus said [Acts 20:35]:

  "It is more blessed to give than to receive."

  How was that true for Jesus who gave it all? What did He receive as He did all this giving? [Discuss.]

  [Hints…]

  - Hebrews 12:2 says that Jesus endured the cross for the "Joy that God put before him." Jesus was filled with joy by obeying the Father and working together with him to complete the work of salvation.
  - Jesus was rewarded and exalted for His generous sacrifice: Philippians 2:9-11:

    "So God raised Christ to the highest place. God made the name of Christ greater than every other name. God wants every knee to bow to Jesus - everyone in heaven, on earth, and under the earth. Everyone will say, "Jesus Christ is Lord" and bring glory to God the Father."

- **Summary Scripture.** The following scripture is so true of both Joseph and Jesus. It actually reads like a story written about their lives. I'm going to read it to you twice. While I read the first time, I'd like you to close your eyes and think about how this was true in the life of Joseph. Let's listen to 2 Corinthians 9:6-11:

"Remember this: The person who plants a little will have a small harvest. But the person who plants a lot will have a big harvest. Each one should give, then, what he has decided in his heart to give. He should not give if it makes him sad. And he should not give if he thinks he is forced to give. God loves the person who gives happily. And God can give you more blessings than you need. Then you will always have plenty of everything. You will have enough to give to every good work. It is written in the Scriptures: 'He gives freely to the poor. The things he does are right and will continue forever.' God is the One who gives seed to the farmer. And he gives bread for food. And God will give you all the seed you need and make it grow. He will make a great harvest from your goodness. God will make you rich in every way so that you can always give freely. And your giving through us will cause many to give thanks to God."

Now, as I read it a second time, please close your eyes and think about how this was true in the life of Jesus. (Reread 2 Corinthians 9:6-11.)

- **Summary Questions.** [Instruct students to give a thumbs up/down sign or shout out yes/no.]
    (1) Does giving make us poorer? *No*
    (2) Is giving a great way to reflect God and work with Him? *Yes*
    (3) Does generosity cause people to give thanks to God? *Yes*
    (4) Is giving money the only way to be generous? *No*
    (5) Do we have a rich identity and purpose which fills us with much to give? *Yes*
    (6) Does giving make us rich with strong relationships? *Yes*
    (7) Are we the true source of what we give to others? *No*

Assign Homework

- **Option A.** Give away something valuable that you would normally have kept for yourself or share a little more than you normally would have. How did this make you feel?

- **Option B.** Use your time, creativity, and hands to make something (picture, story, letter, toy, bracelet, etc.) to give to someone who needs encouragement. Notice how it blesses both him/her and yourself.

Closing Prayer. [If time is short, pray for the students yourself, asking God to help them to grow in generosity. Otherwise, ask students to pray in pairs or small groups that God would help them to become more like the most generous person they know.]

D. Summarizing Identity and Purpose

Requirements.

- **Time.** [The lessons contain roughly 60 minutes of material.]
- **Supplies.** [Paper and colored markers for each student to make a drawing, and copies for each student of How the 12 Truths Have Nourished Your Soul from the Appendix.]

Opening Prayer.

[Write the identity and purpose statements on the whiteboard and pass out copies of How the 12 Truths Have Nourished Your Soul.]

[Two volunteers read identity and purpose statements....]

> "WHO I AM: **I am a cherished child of God with immense value and important responsibility. God gives me joy in healthy relationships with Him, His earth, and other people. God is working to restore me and my relationships to reflect Him beautifully.**"

> "WHY I'M HERE: **God's good plan for me is to nurture the seeds He gives into strong talents to serve Him by serving others. I can be very generous with others because I can trust God to take care of me. He helps my talents bear much fruit that blesses people and God's earth. This pleases the Lord, shows His love to people, and brings me joy. This good work is practice for reigning with Jesus in His Kingdom.**"

What part of these statements mean more to you now than at the beginning of the course? [Discuss.]

[Give students 5 minutes to write answers to the following questions 1-2 from How the 12 Truths Have Nourished Your Soul, then have them discuss for 3 minutes in trios. Then have one student from each trio share with the whole class.

- How has this course changed how you see yourself?
- What beliefs have you added or subtracted?

[Pray to thank God for the ways He has helped your students grow and change.]

[Read each truth, stopping after each one to ask...] How did Joseph live out this truth? [To save time, have one student answer for each of the 12 truths with you filling in any major missing insights.]

Notice how these 12 truths were seeds in Joseph's soul that grew into a fruitful future for him, his family and several whole nations!

Let's look at others in the Bible in which these seeds bore good fruit. How did Jesus live out the five truths about identity? [Discuss.]

Break the class into two groups: boys and girls.

- BOYS – Let's listen to Nehemiah 6…How did Nehemiah live out the 7 truths about purpose? [Discuss after reading.]
- GIRLS – Let's listen to Proverbs 31:10-31… How does the Proverbs 31 woman live out the 7 truths about purpose? [Discuss after reading.]

[Bring the class back together and have 2-3 girls and 2-3 boys share with whole group what they learned.]

[Give students 3 minutes to write answers to the following questions 3-4 from How the 12 Truths Have Nourished Your Soul.]

- Which of these 12 truths have helped you the most and how? [Discuss.]
- Which of these 12 truths do you still struggle to believe or act on?

[Have an adult go around and take legible photographs of completed How the 12 Truths Have Nourished Your Soul forms if students are willing. If possible, please send copies along with a group photo to: info@creatingjobs.org. Thank you!]

[Pass out paper and markers.]

With big, fancy letters, draw out the title of the truth you are struggling with. Add some leaves and flowers to remind you that this truth must grow in your heart from a seed to a mighty tree. We ask that you display your drawing where you can see it every day so it can remind you to embrace this truth completely.

[Break into pairs and have them pray that the truths they've drawn will grow strong in their hearts.]

[Lead class in reading the identity and purpose statements out loud together from the whiteboard.]

[Close in prayer asking God to help students believe and live out these truths and reject these lies.]

[If there are openings in an upcoming Opportunity Makers Course Two, please share the following encouragement to apply.]

It's good to know who you are and why you are here, but unless you let these powerful seeds sprout from your mind into your actions, they cannot produce a fruitful future. There's a big difference between knowing something is true

D. Summarizing Identity and Purpose

and being transformed as it shapes your life. Knowing what a bicycle looks like is vastly inferior to feeling the breeze in your hair as you peddle through a beautiful day!

Recent research shows that you've not completely learned something until you practice it. We already knew this from Bible verses like "faith without work is dead" (James 2:17) and "blessed are those who hear and put into practice these words of mine" (Luke 11:28). For those of you who are serious about living out the 12 truths you've learned in this course, we have a second Opportunity Makers course which you can take. It is called "12 Habits to Co-Create with God". It will help you to integrate your biblical identity and purpose into your daily life. But I must warn you: the commitment is much higher than in Course One. It will be more about what you do in between classes than what happen during class. In fact, it will ask you to change how you spend your time every single day!

That's asking a lot – especially since change is really hard. But because the changes are based on God's Word, they will be very good for you and your future. It's time to let your new beliefs show up in your actions. After learning what a bicycle is and what it does, it's time to hop on and learn to ride it. Yes, it is scary and dangerous, but moving through life in a whole new way will bring you freedom and joy!

Are you ready to see the 12 habits that Course Two will ask you to commit to? [Raise hands.]

Let's read the 12 habits that Course Two will show you how to build into your life.

[Read the 12 habits from page 4 of the Opportunity Makers Overview in the Appendix.]

How interested are you in Course 2? Please hold up one fist. Now raise 1-5 fingers, one meaning "I'm barely interested" and five meaning "I'm very excited about it", with two, three or four fingers being somewhere in between.

[Close in prayer asking God to activate what they've already learned and use Course 2 to put their biblical identity and purpose into further practice.]

APPENDIX

Tools for You and Your Students

Opportunity Makers Overview

These four pages comprise the main resource your students need to bring with them to every lesson. Please print, laminate and bind it into a single resource. You can print it on four 8.5" x 11" pages or on a single 11" x 17" page, if available, folded in half with page one as front cover and page four as back cover. Either laminate or print on waterproof paper. It will look much better in full color, which you can request from info@creatingjobs.org.

Opportunity Makers Overview

Opportunity Makers

24 Seeds for a Fruitful Future

Evan Keller
with Candice Davis & Jeff Hostetter

CreatingJobs.org
Business for Global Good

Purpose of Opportunity Makers:

Nurture the mindset, relationships and habits that can grow a fruitful future in your life and community.

YOU ARE HERE

Course One: *12 Truths to Nourish Your Soul*

Course Two: *12 Habits to Co-Create with God*

"Who Am I?" "Why am I here?"
Course One explores God's answers to life's biggest questions. You'll learn about your biblical identity and purpose from the life of Joseph.

Course One: 12 Truths to Nourish Your Soul

WHO I AM (Identity Statement):

I am a cherished child of God with immense value and important responsibility. God gives me joy in healthy relationships with Him, His earth, and other people. God is working to restore me and my relationships to reflect Him beautifully.

1. I am defined by God's love, not my own thoughts, nor by the actions or words of people. While parents and peers try to shape my self-image, only my Heavenly Father's perspective ultimately matters. When God looks at me, he sees the righteousness of Jesus in whom I trust.

2. God lovingly created me and delights in me. I have immeasurable value because God created me in His image and made me one of His royal representatives. I am a cherished child of a loving Heavenly Father who allowed His Son to die to restore me to Himself.

3. I was created for intimacy, to enjoy harmony with God, people and God's earth. While our sin has damaged all of these relationships, God is working to heal them.

4. God shares my sorrow, gives me strength, and shapes my character when I believe that He is lovingly present in my trials. Even through my hardships, God is working for my good.

5. I am a reflection of God as I cultivate His earth and manage it wisely. My life must show the world what God is like. I do this well as I become more like His Son Jesus.

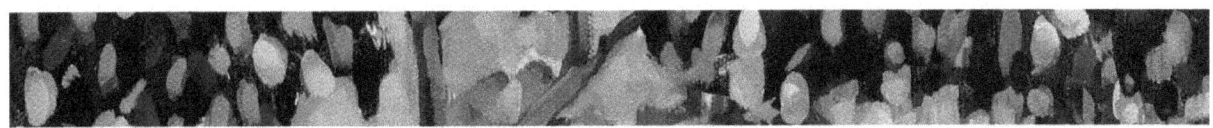

WHY I'M HERE (Purpose Statement):

God's good plan for me is to nurture the seeds He gives into strong talents to serve Him by serving people. I can be very generous with others because I can trust God to take care of me. He helps my gifts bear much fruit to bless people and God's earth. This pleases the Lord, shows His love to others, and brings me joy. This good work is practice for reigning with Jesus in His Kingdom.

6. God has a good plan for my life – to join in his work of making all things right and good. My life and work are to be a small preview of the day when God's Kingdom comes on earth as it is in heaven. Then my cooperation with God will increase – to the point of even reigning with Him!

7. I must develop God's gifts. My life and my gifts are not my own. I have received everything from God. He owns everything and expects me to use everything entrusted to me for His glory. So, I must develop and use these for God: my mind, body, soul, character, time, resources and relationships. God expects me to put these extremely valuable gifts to work to serve Him and my community.

8. Work is a good gift from God to bless people. Working with excellence is a way to worship God and cooperate with Him to serve others. It helps me to imitate God who is a worker and it brings out the usefulness and beauty of His earth. The purpose of my work is to love my neighbors as Jesus commands which brings me joy.

9. I can trust God to work for my good as I focus on obeying His Word. Since my future is secure in God's hands, I can take bold risks to do good today, knowing that all will be well in the end.

10. My actions can really shape the future for me and my community. I am called to make my community better by my godly character and actions. God empowers me to make good things happen as I depend on Him. I can join with others to create new opportunities. Our God-given creativity can conceive them, and our determination can achieve them.

11. I cannot fulfill God's purpose alone, so I must build strong teamwork. We can solve bigger problems together as we rely on other's encouragement, ideas, and God-given abilities. Because God made us for joyful fellowship, our strengths don't merely add together. They multiply when we work together. Even when my teammates do wrong, God can still bring good from it. So, I must work together with others to create good solutions for our community.

12. I should constantly share what God has given me. This is a reflection of God whose grace is always overflowing. God provides for me, so when I share with others, I don't have less. God will continue to bless me so that I can be even more generous. This multiplies joy as generosity strengthens our relationships. We are all grateful to God for His many good gifts.

Course Two: *12 Habits to Co-Create with God*

1. TIME: Spend time wisely.
2. ATTITUDE: Express gratitude and positivity.
3. CARE: Treat people right every time and look out for the vulnerable.
4. DREAMS: Write down your dreams for your family and community.
5. SOLUTIONS: Work with trustworthy friends to solve community problems.
6. DEPENDENCE: Submit your plans to God and ask Him to work through you.
7. INNOVATION: Create and improve things.
8. DISCIPLINE: Do difficult things that over time achieve important goals.
9. FRIENDSHIP: Surround yourself with people of strong character and ambition.
10. GROWTH: Develop your character and keep learning.
11. EXCELLENCE: Develop your gifts and do your very best.
12. MONEY: Maximize your earning, saving, and giving.

Opportunity Makers is offered in partnership between:

Class information and schedule:

Identity Statement

WHO I AM (Identity Statement):

I am a cherished child of God with immense value and important responsibility. God gives me joy in healthy relationships with Him, His earth, and other people. God is working to restore me and my relationships to reflect Him beautifully.

Purpose Statement

WHY I'M HERE (Purpose Statement):

God's good plan for me is to nurture the seeds He gives into strong talents to serve Him by serving people. I can be very generous with others because I can trust God to take care of me. He helps my gifts bear much fruit to bless people and God's earth. This pleases the Lord, shows His love to others, and brings me joy. This good work is practice for reigning with Jesus in His Kingdom.

Truths At-a-Glance

Truths At-a-Glance 131

WHO I AM (Identity Statement):

I am a cherished child of God with immense value and important responsibility. God gives me joy in healthy relationships with Him, His earth, and other people. God is working to restore me and my relationships to reflect Him beautifully.

12 Truths At-a-Glance

1. **DEFINED BY GOD: I am defined by God's love**, not my own thoughts, nor by the actions or words of people.
2. **CHERISHED CHILD: God lovingly created me** and delights in me.
3. **HEALED RELATIONSHIPS: I was created for intimacy**, to enjoy harmony with God, people and God's earth.
4. **PAIN THAT MATURES: God's loving presence in my trials can produce beautiful fruit in my life.**
5. **REFLECTING GOD: I am a reflection of God** as I cultivate His earth and manage it wisely.
6. **GOD'S PLAN: God has a good plan for my life** – to join in His work of making all things right and good.
7. **GOD'S GIFTS: I must develop God's gifts.**
8. **GOOD WORK: Work is a good gift from God** to bless people.
9. **TRUSTING GOD: I can trust God** to work for my good as I focus on obeying His Word.
10. **SHAPING THE FUTURE: My actions can really shape the future** for me and my community.
11. **TEAMWORK: I cannot fulfill God's purpose alone**, so I must build strong teamwork.
12. **GENEROSITY: I should constantly share what God has given me.**

WHY I'M HERE (Purpose Statement):

God's good plan for me is to nurture the seeds He gives into strong talents to serve Him by serving people. I can be very generous with others because I can trust God to take care of me. He helps my gifts bear much fruit to bless people and God's earth. This pleases the Lord, shows His love to others, and brings me joy. This good work is practice for reigning with Jesus in His Kingdom.

Truths and 12 Lies

12 Truths to Nourish Your Soul and 12 Lies That Choke Out Potential.

WHO I AM (Identity Statement): I am a cherished child of God with immense value and important responsibility. God gives me joy in healthy relationships with Him, His creation, and other people. God is working to restore me and my relationships to reflect Him beautifully.

Truths:	Lies:
1. **I am defined by God's love**, not my own thoughts, nor by the actions or words of people. While parents and peers try to shape my self-image, only my Heavenly Father's perspective ultimately matters. When God looks at me, he sees the righteousness of Jesus in whom I trust.	I am defined by my family, home, and possessions. I am lower than others, so I deserve whatever evil is said or done to me. I am unloved and unlovable.
2 **God lovingly created** me and delights in me. I have immeasurable value because God created me in His image and made me one of His royal representatives. I am a cherished child of a loving Heavenly Father who allowed His Son to die to restore me to Himself.	If God even exists, he has forgotten me. I am of little value to anyone. I am worthless. I am no good. I am poor. I am a burden.
3. **I was created for intimacy,** to enjoy harmony with God, people and God's earth. While our sin has damaged all of these relationships, God is working to heal them.	I don't need anyone else. I must look out for myself because people will only harm me. The strong always trample the weak.
4. **God's loving presence in my trials can produce beautiful fruit in my life.** When I realize that God shares my sorrows, He strengthens me and shapes my character. Even through my hardships, God is working for my good.	My sufferings prove that God doesn't care about me. Being cursed and alone makes me bitter and hopeless..
5. **I am a reflection of** God as I cultivate His earth and manage it wisely. My life must show the world what God is like. I do this well as I become more like His Son Jesus.	I am just another animal which has evolved by chance. I have no special identity or role. I am only dust that will return to the earth and be no more.

WHY I'M HERE (Purpose Statement): God's good plan for me is to nurture the seeds He gives into strong talents to serve Him by serving people. I can be very generous with others because I can trust God to take care of me. He helps my gifts bear much fruit to bless people and God's earth. This pleases the Lord, shows His love to others, and brings me joy. This good work is practice for reigning with Jesus in His Kingdom.

Truths:	Lies:
6. God has a good plan for my life – to join in his work of making all things right and good. My life and work are to be a small preview of the day when God's Kingdom comes on earth as it is in heaven. Then my cooperation with God will increase – to the point of even reigning with Him!	**My life has no meaning.** I come from nothing and will go to nothing. I am nothing. The world is no better because I exist. With no reason to serve anyone else, my only purpose is to take whatever I can for myself.
7. I must develop God's gifts. My life and my gifts are not my own. I have received everything from God. He owns everything and expects me to use everything entrusted to me for His glory. So, I must develop and use these for God: my mind, body, soul, character, time, resources and relationships. God expects me to put these extremely valuable gifts to work to serve Him and my community.	**I am empty-handed and have nothing to offer.** I am poor. I am a beggar. The government should help me. The little I do have is mine to spend on myself. I answer to no one. My life is my own. I can do whatever I want with my life. I can ignore my gifts or use them only for myself.
8. Work is a good gift from God to bless people. Working with excellence is a way to worship God and cooperate with Him to serve others. It helps me to imitate God who is a worker and it brings out the usefulness and beauty of His earth. The purpose of my work is to love my neighbors as Jesus commands which brings me joy.	**Work is a curse or a burden.** I should do the minimum amount of work because I get paid so little and my supervisors are not good people. My work is meaningless and always frustrating.
9. I can trust God to work for my good as I focus on obeying His Word. Since my future is secure in God's hands, I can take bold risks to do good today, knowing that all will be well in the end.	**I cannot trust God with my life and future.** He might ask me to do something difficult, and I am afraid I will lose what I already have or suffer the shame of failure. So, I submit to no one. I am my own provider. With no one looking out for me, I must take care of myself. No one else will.

Truths:	Lies:
10. My actions can really shape the future for me and my community. I am called to make my community better by my godly character and actions. God empowers me to make good things happen as I depend on Him. I can join with others to create new opportunities. Our God-given creativity can conceive them, and our determination can achieve them.	**I am a victim.** My negative circumstances define me. Bad people and experiences entrap me. I have no ability to change the future. I must accept my fate. I am trapped in poverty. I have no hope that things will get better. Surviving is my only goal. Dreams of the future are a luxury I cannot afford. I don't have enough money, education, strength, or relationships to pursue dreams that will never come true.
11. I cannot fulfill God's purpose alone, so I must build strong teamwork. We can solve bigger problems together as we rely on other's encouragement, ideas, and God-given abilities. Because God made us for joyful fellowship, our strengths don't merely add together. They multiply when we work together. Even when my teammates do wrong, God can still bring good from it. So, I must work together with others to create good solutions for our community.	**I do not need others since I can do things by myself.** People only hurt me so I should rely on myself alone.
12. I should constantly share what God has given me. This is a reflection of God whose grace is always overflowing. God provides for me, so when I share with others, I don't have less. God will continue to bless me so that I can be even more generous. This multiplies joy as generosity strengthens our relationships. We are all grateful to God for His many good gifts.	**I am crippled by fear of what others will think or do.** Why should I create wealth that others will steal? Why should I share wealth and make myself vulnerable? I must keep my fists closed so I don't lose anything I have worked for.

Supporting Scriptures for 12 Truths

Supporting Scriptures for 12 Truths

WHO I AM (IDENTITY STATEMENT): I am a cherished child of God with immense value and important responsibility. God gives me joy in healthy relationships with Him, His earth, and other people. God is working to restore me and my relationships to reflect Him beautifully.	Supporting Scriptures for 12 Truths
1. DEFINED BY GOD **Truth: I am defined by God's love**, not my own thoughts, nor by the actions or words of people. While parents and peers try to shape my self-image, only my Heavenly Father's perspective ultimately matters. When God looks at me, he sees the righteousness of Jesus in whom I trust. **Lie: I am defined by my family, home, and possessions.** I am lower than others, so I deserve whatever evil is said or done to me. I am unloved and unlovable.	**Psalms 27:10-14** If my father and mother leave me, the Lord will take me in. Lord, teach me your ways. Guide me to do what is right because I have enemies. Do not let my enemies defeat me. They tell lies about me. They say they will hurt me. I truly believe I will live to see the Lord's goodness. Wait for the Lord's help. Be strong and brave and wait for the Lord's help. **Romans 8:31** So, what should we say about this? If God is for us, then no one can defeat us. **Ephesians 2:4-5** But God's mercy is great, and he loved us very much. We were spiritually dead because of the things we did wrong against God. But God gave us new life with Christ. You have been saved by God's grace.
2. CHERISHED CHILD **Truth: God lovingly created me** and delights in me. I have immeasurable value because God created me in His image and made me one of His royal representatives. I am a cherished child of a loving	**Psalms 139:13-14** You made my whole being. You formed me in my mother's body. I praise you because you made me in an amazing and wonderful way. What you have done is wonderful. I know this very well. **Romans 8:14-19** The Spirit that we have makes us children of God. And with that Spirit we say, "Father, dear Father." And the Spirit himself joins with our spirits to say that we are God's children. If we are God's children, then we will

Heavenly Father who allowed His Son to die to restore me to Himself.

Lie: If God even exists, he has forgotten me. I am of little value to anyone. I am worthless. I am no good. I am poor. I am a burden.

---

receive the blessings God has for us. We will receive these things from God together with Christ. But we must suffer as Christ

suffered, and then we will have glory as Christ has glory. We have sufferings now. But the sufferings we have now are nothing compared to the great glory that will be given to us. Everything that God made is waiting with excitement for the time when God will show the world who his children are. The whole world wants very much for that to happen.

Romans 8:32
God let even his own Son suffer for us. God gave his Son for us all. So with Jesus, God will surely give us all things.

Ephesians 5:1-2
You are God's children whom he loves. So try to be like God. Live a life of love. Love other people just as Christ loved us. Christ gave himself for us—he was a sweet-smelling offering and sacrifice to God.

---

3. HEALED RELATIONSHIPS

Truth: I was created for intimacy, to enjoy harmony with God, people and God's earth. While our sin has damaged all of these relationships, God is working to heal them.

Lie: I don't need anyone else. I must look out for myself because people will only harm me. The strong always trample the weak.

Genesis 2:18
Then the Lord God said, "It is not good for the man to be alone. I will make a helper who is right for him."

Genesis 3:8
Then they heard the Lord God walking in the garden. This was during the cool part of the day. And the man and his wife hid from the Lord God among the trees in the garden.

Genesis 3:16-19a
Then God said to the woman, "I will cause you to have much trouble when you are pregnant. And when you give birth to children, you will have great pain. You will greatly desire your husband, but he will rule over you." Then God said to the man, "You listened to what your wife said. And you ate fruit from the tree that I commanded you not to eat from. "So I will put a curse on the ground. You will have to work very hard for food. In pain you will eat its food all the days of your life. The ground will produce thorns and weeds for you. And you will eat the plants of the field. You will sweat and work hard for your food.

	Malachi 4:6 Elijah will help fathers love their children. And he will help the children love their fathers. Otherwise, I will come and put a curse on the land." **Luke 19:1-10** (Please look up this story of Jesus & Zacchaeus.) **Romans 12:17-19** If someone does wrong to you, do not pay him back by doing wrong to him. Try to do what everyone thinks is right. Do your best to live in peace with everyone. My friends, do not try to punish others when they wrong you. Wait for God to punish them with his anger. It is written: "I am the One who punishes; I will pay people back," says the Lord. **1 Peter 3:8-9** Finally, all of you should live together in peace. Try to understand each other. Love each other as brothers. Be kind and humble. Do not do wrong to a person to pay him back for doing wrong to you. Or do not insult someone to pay him back for insulting you. But ask God to bless that person. Do this, because you yourselves were called to receive a blessing.

4. PAIN THAT MATURES
 	
Truth: God's loving presence in my trials can produce beautiful fruit in my life. When I realize that God shares my sorrows, He strengthens me and shapes my character. Even through my hardships, God is working for my good.
 	
Lie: My sufferings prove that God doesn't care about me. Being cursed and alone makes me bitter and hopeless.
	Psalm 34:18
	The Lord is close to the brokenhearted.
	   He saves those whose spirits have been crushed.
	
	Isaiah 43:2
	When you pass through the waters, I will be with you.
	   When you cross rivers, you will not drown.
	When you walk through fire, you will not be burned.
	   The flames will not hurt you.
	
	Isaiah 53:4a
	But he took our suffering on him and felt our pain for us.
	
	Isaiah 63:9
	When they suffered, he suffered also.
	   He sent his own angel to save them.
	Because of his love and kindness, the Lord saved them.
	   Since long ago he has picked them up and carried them.

John 11:32-36
But Mary went to the place where Jesus was. When she saw him, she fell at his feet and said, "Lord, if you had been here, my brother would

not have died." Jesus saw that Mary was crying and that the Jews who came with her were crying, too. Jesus felt very sad in his heart and was deeply troubled. He asked, "Where did you bury him?" "Come and see, Lord," they said. Jesus cried. So the Jews said, "See how much he loved him."

John 15:1-2,5
I am the true vine; my Father is the gardener. He cuts off every branch of mine that does not produce fruit. And he trims and cleans every branch that produces fruit so that it will produce even more fruit....I am the vine, and you are the branches. If a person remains in me and I remain in him, then he produces much fruit. But without me he can do nothing.

John 16:33
"I told you these things so that you can have peace in me. In this world you will have trouble. But be brave! I have defeated the world!"

Acts 7:54-60
When the leaders heard Stephen saying all these things, they became very angry. They were so mad that they were grinding their teeth at Stephen. But Stephen was full of the Holy Spirit. He looked up to heaven and saw the glory of God. He saw Jesus standing at God's right side. He said, "Look! I see heaven open. And I see the Son of Man standing at God's right side!" Then they all shouted loudly.

They covered their ears with their hands and all ran at Stephen. They took him out of the city and threw stones at him until he was dead. The men who told lies against Stephen left their coats with a young man named Saul. While they were throwing stones, Stephen prayed, "Lord Jesus, receive my spirit!" He fell on his knees and cried in a loud voice, "Lord, do not hold this sin against them!" After Stephen said this, he died.

Romans 5:3-5
And we also have joy with our troubles because we know that these troubles produce patience. And patience produces character, and character produces hope. And this hope will never disappoint us,

because God has poured out his love to fill our hearts. God gave us his love through the Holy Spirit, whom God has given to us.

Romans 8:28, 31-32
We know that in everything God works for the good of those who love him. They are the people God called, because that was his plan....If God is for us, then no one can defeat us. God let even his own Son suffer for us. God gave his Son for us all. So with Jesus, God will surely give us all things.

Romans 8:35-39
Can anything separate us from the love Christ has for us? Can troubles or problems or sufferings? If we have no food or clothes, if we are in danger, or even if death comes—can any of these things separate us from Christ's love? As it is written in the Scriptures:
"For you we are in danger of death all the time.
   People think we are worth no more than sheep to be killed."

But in all these things we have full victory through God who showed his love for us. Yes, I am sure that nothing can separate us from the love God has for us. Not death, not life, not angels, not ruling spirits, nothing now, nothing in the future, no powers, nothing above us, nothing below us, or anything else in the whole world will ever be able to separate us from the love of God that is in Christ Jesus our Lord.

James 1:2-4
My brothers, you will have many kinds of troubles. But when these things happen, you should be very happy. You know that these things are testing your faith. And this will give you patience. Let your patience show itself perfectly in what you do. Then you will be perfect and complete. You will have everything you need.

5. REFLECTING GOD

Truth: I am a reflection of God as I cultivate his earth and manage it wisely. My life must show the world what God is like. I do this well as I become more like His Son Jesus.

Lie: I am just another animal which has evolved by chance. I have no special identity or role. I am only dust that will return to the earth and be no more.

Genesis 1:26-28
Then God said, "Let us make human beings in our image and likeness. And let them rule over the fish in the sea and the birds in the sky. Let them rule over the tame animals, over all the earth and over all the small crawling animals on the earth." So God created human beings in his image. In the image of God he created them. He created them male and female. God blessed them and said, "Have many children and grow in

number. Fill the earth and be its master. Rule over the fish in the sea and over the birds in the sky. Rule over every living thing that moves on the earth."

Isaiah 60:1-3
"Jerusalem, get up and shine. Your light has come. The glory of the Lord shines on you. Darkness now covers the earth. Deep darkness covers her people. But the Lord shines on you, and people see his glory around you. Nations will come to your light. Kings will come to the brightness of your sunrise."

Romans 8:29
God knew them before he made the world. And God chose them to be like his Son. Then Jesus would be the firstborn of many brothers.

2 Corinthians 3:18
Our faces, then, are not covered. We all show the Lord's glory, and we are being changed to be like him. This change in us brings more and more glory. And it comes from the Lord, who is the Spirit.

Galatians 4:19
My little children, again I feel pain for you as a mother feels when she gives birth. I will feel this until you truly become like Christ.

WHY I'M HERE (PURPOSE STATEMENT): God's good plan for me is to nurture the seeds He gives into strong talents to serve Him by serving people. I can be very generous with others because I can trust God to take care of me. He helps my gifts bear much fruit to bless people and God's earth. This pleases the Lord, shows His love to others, and brings me joy. This good work is practice for reigning with Jesus in His Kingdom.	Supporting Scriptures
6. GOD'S PLAN **Truth: God has a good plan for my life** – to join in his work of making all things right and good. My life and work are to be a small preview of the day when God's Kingdom comes on earth as it is in heaven. Then my cooperation with God will increase – to the point of even reigning with Him! **Lie: My life has no meaning.** I come from nothing and will go to nothing. I am nothing. The world is no better because I exist. With no reason to serve anyone else, my only purpose is to take whatever I can for myself.	**Genesis 2:19-20** From the ground God formed every wild animal and every bird in the sky. He brought them to the man so the man could name them. Whatever the man called each living thing, that became its name. The man gave names to all the tame animals, to the birds in the sky and to all the wild animals. **Psalms 8:3-9** I look at the heavens, which you made with your hands. I see the moon and stars, which you created. But why is man important to you? Why do you take care of human beings? You made man a little lower than the angels. And you crowned him with glory and honor. You put him in charge of everything you made. You put all things under his control: all the sheep, the cattle and the wild animals, the birds in the sky, the fish in the sea, and everything that lives under water. Lord our Master, your name is the most wonderful name in all the earth! **Jeremiah 29:11** "I say this because I know what I have planned for you," says the Lord. "I have good plans for you. I don't plan to hurt you. I plan to give you hope and a good future."

John 4:34
Jesus said, "My food is to do what the One who sent me wants me to do. My food is to finish the work that he gave me to do.

1 Corinthians 3:9
For we are God's coworkers.

2 Timothy 2:20-21
In a large house there are things made of gold and silver. But also there are things made of wood and clay. Some things are used for special purposes, and others are made for ordinary jobs. If anyone makes himself clean from evil things, he will be used for special purposes. He will be made holy, and the Master can use him. He will be ready to do any good work.

Revelations 5:9-10
And they all sang a new song to the Lamb: "You are worthy to take the scroll and to open its seals, because you were killed; and with the blood of your death you bought men for God from every tribe, language, people, and nation. You made them to be a kingdom of priests for our God. And they will rule on the earth."

---

7. GOD'S GIFTS

Truth: I must develop God's gifts. My life and my gifts are not my own. I have received everything from God. He owns everything and expects me to use everything entrusted to me for His glory. So, I must develop and use these for God: my mind, body, soul, character, time, resources and relationships. God expects me to put these extremely valuable gifts to work to serve my community.

Lie: I am empty-handed and have nothing to offer. I am poor. I am a

Exodus 31:1-5
Then the Lord said to Moses, "See, I have chosen Bezalel son of Uri from the tribe of Judah. Uri was the son of Hur. I have filled Bezalel with the Spirit of God. I have given him the skill, ability and knowledge to do all kinds of work. He is able to design pieces to be made from gold, silver and bronze. He is able to cut jewels and put them in metal. And he can carve wood. Bezalel can do all kinds of work.

Matthew 25:14-30 (Please look up parable of Jesus.)

Luke 2:52
Jesus continued to learn more and more and to grow physically. People liked him, and he pleased God.

Luke 12:48b
"Everyone who has been given much will be responsible for much. Much more will be expected from the one who has been given more."

Supporting Scriptures for 12 Truths   149

beggar. The government should help me. The little I do have is mine to spend on myself. I answer to no one; my life is my own. I can do whatever I want with my life. I can ignore my gifts or use them only for myself.	**1 Corinthians 4:7** Everything you have was given to you. And if this is so, why do you brag as if you got these things by your own power? **1 Corinthians 6:19** You should know that your body is a temple for the Holy Spirit. The Holy Spirit is in you. You have received the Holy Spirit from God. You do not own yourselves. **Ephesians 5:15-16** So be very careful how you live. Do not live like those who are not wise. Live wisely. I mean that you should use every chance you have for doing good, because these are evil times. **Hebrews 13:20-21** I pray that the God of peace will give you every good thing you need so that you can do what he wants. God is the One who raised from death our Lord Jesus, the Great Shepherd of the sheep. God raised him because of the blood of his death. His blood began the agreement that God made with his people. And this agreement is eternal. I pray that God, through Christ, will do in us what pleases him. And to Jesus Christ be glory forever and ever. Amen. **1 Peter 4:10** Each of you received a spiritual gift. God has shown you his grace in giving you different gifts. And you are like servants who are responsible for using God's gifts. So be good servants and use your gifts to serve each other.
8. GOOD WORK **Truth: Work is a good gift from God** to bless people. Working with excellence is a way to worship God and cooperate with Him to serve others. It helps me to imitate God who is a worker and it brings out the	**Genesis 1:31** God looked at everything he had made, and it was very good. Evening passed, and morning came. This was the sixth day. **Genesis 2:19-20a** From the ground God formed every wild animal and every bird in the sky. He brought them to the man so the man could name them. Whatever the man called each living thing, that became its name. The

usefulness and beauty of His earth. The purpose of my work is to love my neighbors as Jesus commands which brings me joy.

Lie: Work is a curse or a burden. I should do the minimum amount of work because I get paid so little and my supervisors are not good people. My work is meaningless and always frustrating.

man gave names to all the tame animals, to the birds in the sky and to all the wild animals.

Deuteronomy 8:18a (NIV)
But remember the LORD your God, for it is he who gives you the ability to produce wealth.

Proverbs 14:23
Those who work hard make a profit. But those who only talk will be poor.

Proverbs 18:9
A person who doesn't work hard is just like a person who destroys things.

Proverbs 22:29
Do you see a man skilled in his work? That man will work for kings. He won't have to work for ordinary people.

Mark 12:31a
The second most important command is this: 'Love your neighbor as you love yourself.'

1 Corinthians 3:9a (ESV)
For we are God's fellow workers.

Colossians 3:23-24
In all the work you are doing, work the best you can. Work as if you were working for the Lord, not for men. Remember that you will receive your reward from the Lord, which he promised to his people. You are serving the Lord Christ.

2 Timothy 2:15
Do the best you can to be the kind of person that God will approve, and give yourself to him. Be a worker who is not ashamed of his work—a worker who uses the true teaching in the right way.

9. TRUSTING GOD

Truth: I can trust God to work for my good as I focus on obeying His Word. Since my future is secure in God's hands, I can take bold risks to do good today, knowing that all will be well in the end.

Lie: I cannot trust God with my life and future. He might ask me to do something difficult, and I am afraid I will lose what I already have or suffer the shame of failure. So, I submit to no one. I am my own provider. With no one looking out for me, I must take care of myself. No one else will.

Joshua 1:9
"Remember that I commanded you to be strong and brave. So don't be afraid. The Lord your God will be with you everywhere you go."

Psalm 23:4
Even if I walk through a very dark valley, I will not be afraid because you are with me.

Psalm 84:5-7
Happy are those whose strength comes from you. They want to travel to Jerusalem. As they pass through the Valley of Baca, they make it like a spring. The autumn rains fill it with pools of water. The people get stronger as they go. And everyone meets with God in Jerusalem.

Psalms 84:11-12
The Lord God is like our sun and shield. The Lord gives us kindness and glory. He does not hold back anything good from those whose life is innocent.
Lord of heaven's armies, happy are the people who trust you!

Proverbs 3:5-6
Trust the Lord with all your heart.
   Don't depend on your own understanding.
Remember the Lord in everything you do.
   And he will give you success.

Matthew 6:33
"The thing you should want most is God's kingdom and doing what God wants. Then all these other things you need will be given to you."

Luke 22:42-44
"Father, if it is what you want, then let me not have this cup of suffering. But do what you want, not what I want." Then an angel from heaven appeared to him to help him. Jesus was full of pain; he prayed even more. Sweat dripped from his face as if he were bleeding.

Romans 8:28
We know that in everything God works for the good of those who love him. They are the people God called, because that was his plan.

1 Peter 2:23
People insulted Christ, but he did not insult them in return. Christ suffered, but he did not threaten. He let God take care of him. God is the One who judges rightly.

1 Peter 4:19
So then those who suffer as God wants them to should trust their souls to him. God is the One who made them, and they can trust him. So they should continue to do what is right.

10. SHAPING THE FUTURE

Truth: My actions can really shape the future for me and my community. I am called to make my community better by my godly character and actions. God empowers me to make good things happen as I depend on Him. I can join with others to create new opportunities. Our God-given creativity can conceive them, and our determination can achieve them.

Lie: I am a victim. My negative circumstances define me. Bad people and experiences entrap me. I have no ability to change the future. I must accept my fate. I am trapped in poverty. I have no hope that things will get better. Surviving is my only goal. Dreams of the future are a luxury I cannot afford. I don't have enough money, education, strength, or relationships to pursue dreams that will never come true.

Proverbs 11:10-11
When good people succeed, the city is happy. When evil people die, there are shouts of joy. The influence of good people makes a city great. But the wicked can destroy it with their words.

Jeremiah 29:11
"I say this because I know what I have planned for you," says the Lord. "I have good plans for you. I don't plan to hurt you. I plan to give you hope and a good future."

Luke 6:38
"Give, and you will receive. You will be given much. It will be poured into your hands—more than you can hold. You will be given so much that it will spill into your lap. The way you give to others is the way God will give to you."

1 Corinthians 3:9-14
We are workers together for God. And you are like a farm that belongs to God. And you are a house that belongs to God. Like an expert builder I built the foundation of that house. I used the gift that God gave me to do this. Others are building on that foundation. But everyone should be careful how he builds. The foundation has already been built. No one can build any other foundation. The foundation that has already been laid is Jesus Christ. Anyone can build on that foundation, using gold, silver, jewels, wood, grass, or straw. But the work that each person does will be clearly seen, because the Day will make it plain. That Day will appear with fire, and the fire will test every man's work. If the building that a man puts on the foundation still stands, he will get his reward.

Supporting Scriptures for 12 Truths

Colossians 1:29
To do this, I work and struggle, using Christ's great strength that works so powerfully in me.

Titus 3:14
Our people must learn to use their lives for doing good deeds. They should do good to those in need. Then our people will not have useless lives.

11. TEAMWORK

Truth: I cannot fulfill God's purpose alone, so I must build strong teamwork. We can solve bigger problems together as we rely on other's encouragement, ideas, and God-given abilities. Because God made us for joyful fellowship, our strengths don't merely *add* together. They *multiply* when we work together. Even when my teammates do wrong, God can still bring good from it. So, I must work together with others to create good solutions for our community.

Lie: I cannot trust anyone. I do not need others since I can do things by myself. People only hurt me so I should rely on myself alone.

Genesis 50:20-21
"You meant to hurt me. But God turned your evil into good. It was to save the lives of many people. And it is being done. So don't be afraid. I will take care of you and your children." So Joseph comforted his brothers and spoke kind words to them.

Ecclesiastes 4:9-12
Two people are better than one.
  They get more done by working together.
If one person falls, the other can help him up.
But it is bad for the person who is alone when he falls.
  No one is there to help him.
If two lie down together, they will be warm.
  But a person alone will not be warm.
An enemy might defeat one person,
  but two people together can defend themselves.
A rope that has three parts wrapped together
  is hard to break.

Romans 15:5-7
Patience and encouragement come from God. And I pray that God will help you all agree with each other the way Christ Jesus wants. Then you will all be joined together, and you will give glory to God the Father of our Lord Jesus Christ. Christ accepted you, so you should accept each other. This will bring glory to God.

1 Corinthians 12:19-21,27
If each part of the body were the same part, there would be no body. But truly God put the parts in the body as he wanted them. He made a place for each one of them. And so there are many parts, but only one body.

	The eye cannot say to the hand, "I don't need you!" And the head cannot say to the foot, "I don't need you!" ....All of you together are the body of Christ. Each one of you is a part of that body.

12. GENEROSITY
 	
Truth: I should constantly share what God has given me. This is a reflection of God whose grace is always overflowing. God provides for me, so when I share with others, I don't have less. God will continue to bless me so that I can be even more generous. This multiplies joy as generosity strengthens our relationships. We are all grateful to God for His many good gifts.
 	
Lie: I am crippled by fear of what others will think or do. Why should I create wealth that others will steal? Why should I share wealth and make myself vulnerable? I must keep my fists closed so I don't lose anything I have worked for.
	1 Chronicles 29:14
	"These things did not really come from me and my people.
	    Everything comes from you.
	    We have given you back what you gave us."
	
	Proverbs 11:24-25
	Some people give much but get back even more.
	    But others don't give what they should, and they end up poor.
	A person who gives to others will get richer.
	    Whoever helps others will himself be helped.
	
	Isaiah 58:10-11
	You should feed those who are hungry.
	    You should take care of the needs of those who are troubled.
	Then your light will shine in the darkness.
	    And you will be bright like sunshine at noon.
	The Lord will always lead you.
	    He will satisfy your needs in dry lands.
	    He will give strength to your bones.
	You will be like a garden that has much water.
	    You will be like a spring that never runs dry.
	
	Luke 6:35,38
	So love your enemies. Do good to them, and lend to them without hoping to get anything back. If you do these things, you will have a great reward. You will be sons of the Most High God. Yes, because God is kind even to people who are ungrateful and full of sin...."Give, and you will receive. You will be given much. It will be poured into your hands—more than you can hold. You will be given so much that it will spill into your lap. The way you give to others is the way God will give to you."
	
	Acts 20:35
	"I showed you in all things that you should work as I did and help the weak. I taught you to remember the words of Jesus. He said, 'It is more blessed to give than to receive.'"

1 Corinthians 4:7
Everything you have was given to you. And if this is so, why do you brag as if you got these things by your own power?

2 Corinthians 9:6-11
Remember this: The person who plants a little will have a small harvest. But the person who plants a lot will have a big harvest. Each one should give, then, what he has decided in his heart to give. He should not give if it makes him sad. And he should not give if he thinks he is forced to give. God loves the person who gives happily. And God can give you more blessings than you need. Then you will always have plenty of everything. You will have enough to give to every good work.

It is written in the Scriptures: "He gives freely to the poor. The things he does are right and will continue forever." God is the One who gives seed to the farmer. And he gives bread for food. And God will give you all the seed you need and make it grow. He will make a great harvest from your goodness. God will make you rich in every way so that you can always give freely. And your giving through us will cause many to give thanks to God.

Hebrews 12:2
Let us look only to Jesus. He is the one who began our faith, and he makes our faith perfect. Jesus suffered death on the cross. But he accepted the shame of the cross as if it were nothing. He did this because of the joy that God put before him. And now he is sitting at the right side of God's throne.

How Joseph Embodied the 12 Truths and Resisted the 12 Lies

How Joseph Embodied the 12 Truths:	How Joseph Resisted the 12 Lies:
Truth 1. I am defined by God's love, not by own thoughts, nor by the actions or words of people. • Confidence from God-given dreams may have strengthened him to endure the hate of his brothers and mistreatment in Egypt.	**Lie 1. I am defined by my family, home and possessions.** • Coat of many colors led to pride. • Being his father's favorites led to pride.
Truth 2. God lovingly created me and delights in me. • His father's love - however marred - reflected God's. • Royal representative of God & the King. • Gained strength from God's presence.	**Lie 2. If God exists, he has forgotten me.** • Seemed like true at several points. • Likely tempted to feel worthless when tossed like garbage into a pit and later a dungeon.
Truth 3. I was created for intimacy, to enjoy harmony with God, people, and God's earth. • The Lord was with him. • He sought reconciliation, not revenge. • His planning enabled harmony with God's earth.	**Lie 3. I don't need anyone else.** • Seemed true in pit and jail. • Didn't lose confidence in long trials because he drew strength from God's presence. • Sought help from cup bearer.
Truth 4. God's loving presence in my trials can produce beautiful fruit in my life. • He was transformed from boastful kid to self-controlled and trusting of God. • Drew strength from God's presence - believing in God's good purpose even when present circumstances looked hopeless. • Endured 13 years of suffering.	**Lie 4. My sufferings prove that God doesn't care about me.** • He didn't lose hope or become bitter when facing betrayal, slavery, false accusation, and abandonment for 13 years. • Even before being enslaved, he'd been motherless for several years. • Joseph's father Jacob's was tempted by this lie in 42:36,38 even though Joseph had suffered more than he.

Truth 5. I am a reflection of God as I cultivate His earth and manage it wisely. • He used his gifts of planning, leadership and closeness to God (by which he interpreted dreams) to earn the trust of the king and he revealed God's wisdom by being used of God to feed the world. • Showed the king and Egypt the power and love of God.	**Lie 5. I am just another animal which has evolved by chance.** • Although he was treated like an animal at times, he lived with dignity of one who bears God's image.
Truth 6. God has a good plan for my life - to join in his work of making all things right and good. • Only after difficult years did it become clear that God had a purpose in his hardships – to save the world from famine. • Reigning with Pharaoh is a picture of how God trusts us to use his good gifts to improve our communities. • Joseph's one little life had an important role in God's work in the world – the same is true of us. • Joseph worked to make life better for himself and all around him.	**Lie 6. My life has no meaning.** • Could have killed himself. • Could have stolen Potiphar's possessions and wife. • Could have said: "I have been taken advantage of – now it's my turn." Instead, he broke the cycle of his conniving father by trusting God to take care of him (instead of scheming to gain advantage).
Truth 7. I must develop God's gifts. • Learned, planned, and built relationships to help put his gifts to work (41:45). • Even though he was a "daddy's boy" who likely wasn't even fully trained as a shepherd, he figured out how to manage an entire estate, then an entire prison, and then an entire country-wide agriculture department. • This required lots of learning, planning, experimenting, effort and perseverance.	**Lie 7. I am empty-handed and have nothing to offer.** • Could have easily felt sorry for himself since no one but God was there to encourage and motivate him. Could have developed gifts, relationships, and resources to plan revenge against his brothers.

<ul><li>He developed himself to solve problems which others came to value highly.</li></ul>Depended on God to interpret 40:8, 41:16 whereas the King's magicians failed.	
Truth 8. Work is a good gift from God to bless people. <ul><li>Five times the Bible says that Potiphar put Joseph in charge.</li><li>39: 22-24: God gave him success in his work that earned the trust of his employers.</li><li>In 39:22 Joseph took "care of all the prisoners". The jailor saw that Joseph was good at serving others. Each of his "employers" saw his responsibility and hard work which led them to promote him with more responsibility and authority.</li><li>He found satisfaction in doing good work even though not being paid *at all* (until becoming prime minister) and was separated from his family and home.</li><li>Like God, he created wealth that blessed others.</li><li>Was wise steward of abundance of God's earth.</li></ul>	**Lie 8. Work is a curse or a burden.** <ul><li>A tempting thought since his pay was zero, but instead he was working for God.</li></ul>He could have done the minimum to stay out of trouble instead of genuinely seeking the good of those who were over him.
Truth 9. I can trust God to work for my good as I focus on obeying His Word. <ul><li>Obeyed God's Word: "How can I do such an evil thing: it is a sin against God" (39:8).</li><li>Obeyed God's command not to take another man's wife.</li><li>Ran from evil (39:12). Refusing Potiphar's wife was risky, but he chose to trust God and do what was right.</li><li>It took courage to interpret a dream for the king.</li><li>Took on big challenge of producing and saving food for seven years.</li></ul>	**Lie 9. I cannot trust God with my life and future.** <ul><li>Could've said: "I've been burned when doing things right (working hard, not taking Potiphar's wife), so now that I'm my own boss – I'll put myself first."</li></ul>Could've bargained or extorted with his gift of interpretation.

• Left his own future to God – was faithful instead of rebellious during a *long* wait.	
Truth 10. My actions can really shape the future for me and my community. • Using his gifts of discernment and leadership, he saved the world. • He leaned on God for strength. • God used him to shape the future for a whole country after he had been faithful in smaller responsibilities in the past. • He created wealth for the hungry and the king. • God gave him wisdom that leaders recognized and influenced them to "put him in charge": 41:33-43.	**Lie 10. I am a victim.** • He thought about the future. For example: his and others dreams, asked the cup bearer to "remember me", and worked faithfully to earn more responsibility and authority in the future. • Others would have let their spirits be broken and given up, maybe even taken their own lives. • He saw that his present situation didn't point to a bright future, but knew God was with him. • His father Jacob had a victim attitude in 42:36,38 even though Joseph had suffered more than he.
Truth 11. I cannot fulfill God's purpose alone. • Gave his extra effort (to Potiphar and jailer) with no promise of reward. • Trusted God to right wrongs: brothers, Potiphar's wife, and cup bearer (whose forgetfulness in 42:23 caused two more years of unjust suffering at first, but this delay later caused the timing to be right to help the king). • Was slow to learn this with his brothers, bringing a bad report (37:2) instead of fostering teamwork. • Experienced this scripture: "Give & shall be given unto you" by making life better for Potiphar, the cup bearer, and the king. • Worked together with farmers and officials to create abundance. • Generous with his effort and interpretations to build goodwill.	**Lie 11. I do not need others since I can do things by myself.** Didn't hoard his interpretive gift.

• Gave his brothers money in their sacks and other gifts.	
Truth 12. I should constantly share what God has given me. • God blessed Potiphar's household because of Joseph. • The more he blessed others, the more God blessed him, but it was a long time of sowing before his harvest. • His good management of the grain led to a reunion with his family and much joy. • God made him succeed in everything: 39:23.	**Lie 12. I am crippled by fear of what others will think or do.** He could've kept the king's interpretation to himself or lied about its meaning, thinking: "These dirty foreigners have kept me imprisoned without cause for 13 years. Why should I help them? I can say something to get out of prison, then go tell my family that God is sending seven fat years then seven lean years."

Time Line of Joseph's Life

Timeline of Joseph's Life

At age...	Joseph...
0	born in Paddan Aram - 11th of 12 sons.
6	travels to Canaan with his family.
8-12?	mother Rachel dies.
14-16?	has strange dreams and father gives him a coat of many colors.
17	sold by brothers into slavery in Egypt.
17	enslaved by Potiphar, captain of the guard of Egypt.
19-20	excels and is put in charge of Potiphar's entire household and farm.
20-24?	imprisoned after being accused by Potiphar's wife.
24-27?	excels and is put in charge of entire prison.
28	interprets dreams for the King's cup bearer and baker.
30	interprets dreams for King and becomes second in command.
30	marries Asenath.
30-36	becomes father to Manasseh and Ephraim.
30-36	oversees storing of grain during seven years of plenty.
37-43	oversees distribution of grain during seven years of famine.
39	brothers make first journey from Canaan to buy grain from Joseph.
41	reveals himself to his brothers and reconciles with them.
42	father, brothers and entire extended family moves from Canaan to Egypt.
56	father Jacob blesses him, calling him a fruitful vine fed by a spring.
56	father Jacob dies at age 147; reassures his brother that he forgives them.
110	dies in Egypt.

Truth Lesson Outline

Truth Lesson Outline

FIRST HALF – 45 minutes

Review Previous Lesson's Homework. [Have each adult lead a small group of students in sharing how their homework went. Adults record who did their homework as credit toward graduation.]

Share the title of today's lesson and how it fits into the course as a whole. [Review with students the "Opportunity Makers Overview" from the Appendix to remind them of how today's lesson connects to what they have been learning. For example remind them of the Identity Statement (for lessons 1-5) or Purpose Statement (for lessons 6-12) and the truths from previous lessons. If possible, show these things on the whiteboard as well.]

Opening Prayer.

Student Activity.

- Explain.
- Do.
- Debrief.

Teach the Truth and Lie.

- **Transition.**
- **Read the Truth and Lie.** Today's entire lesson is built upon this biblical truth. Please read it aloud with me [from whiteboard or poster on wall where students can be reminded of the topic throughout the lesson].
- **Explain.** [Explain the truth further in your own words if necessary.]
- **Support with Scripture.**
- **Illustrate.**

Example of Joseph.

- **Transition.**
- **Read from Genesis.**
- **Discuss.**

Closing Prayer. [Thank God for key biblical insights uncovered during the lesson.]

Truth Lesson Outline

SECOND HALF – 45 minutes

Opening Prayer.

Re-read Truth and Lie.

Imagination Exercise.

- Directions.
- Read from Genesis.
- Discuss.

Summary.

- **Summary Statement.**
- **Example of Jesus.**
- **Summary Scripture.**
- **Summary Questions.** [Instruct students to give a thumbs up/down sign or shout out yes/no.]

Assign Homework.

- Option A.
- Option B.

Closing Prayer. [If time is short, pray for the students. Otherwise, ask students to pray in pairs or small groups.]

How the 12 Truths Nourished Your Soul

How the 12 Truths Have Nourished Your Soul

Name: _____ Date: _____ Location: _____

- How has this course changed how you see yourself? _____
  _____
  _____

- What beliefs have you added or subtracted? _____
  _____
  _____

- Which of the 12 truths have helped you the most and how? (See below and write the numbers here.) _____
  _____
  _____

- Which of the below 12 truths do you still struggle to believe or act on? (See below and write the numbers here.)
  _____

1. DEFINED BY GOD:	**I am defined by God's love**, not my own thoughts, nor by the actions or words of people.
2. CHERISHED CHILD:	**God lovingly created me** and delights in me.
3. HEALED RELATIONSHIPS:	**I was created for intimacy**, to enjoy harmony with God, people and God's earth.
4. PAIN THAT MATURES:	**God shares my sorrow**, gives me strength, and shapes my character when I believe that He is lovingly present in my trials.
5. REFLECTING GOD:	**I am a reflection of God** as I cultivate His earth and manage it wisely.
6. GOD'S PLAN:	**God has a good plan for my life** – to join in His work of making all things right and good.
7. GOD'S GIFTS:	**I must develop God's gifts.**
8. GOOD WORK:	**Work is a good gift from God** to bless others.
9. TRUST IN GOD:	**I can trust God** to work for my good as I focus on obeying His Word.
10. SHAPING THE FUTURE:	**My actions can really shape the future** for me and my community.
11. TEAMWORK:	**I cannot fulfill God's purpose alone**, so I must build strong teamwork.
12. GENEROSITY:	**I should constantly share what God has given me.**

Image of the Moon

Image of the Moon

Image of Grape Vine with Fruit

Image of Grape Vine with Fruit

Image of Birds Flying in a "V" Formation

Image of Birds Flying in a "V" Formation

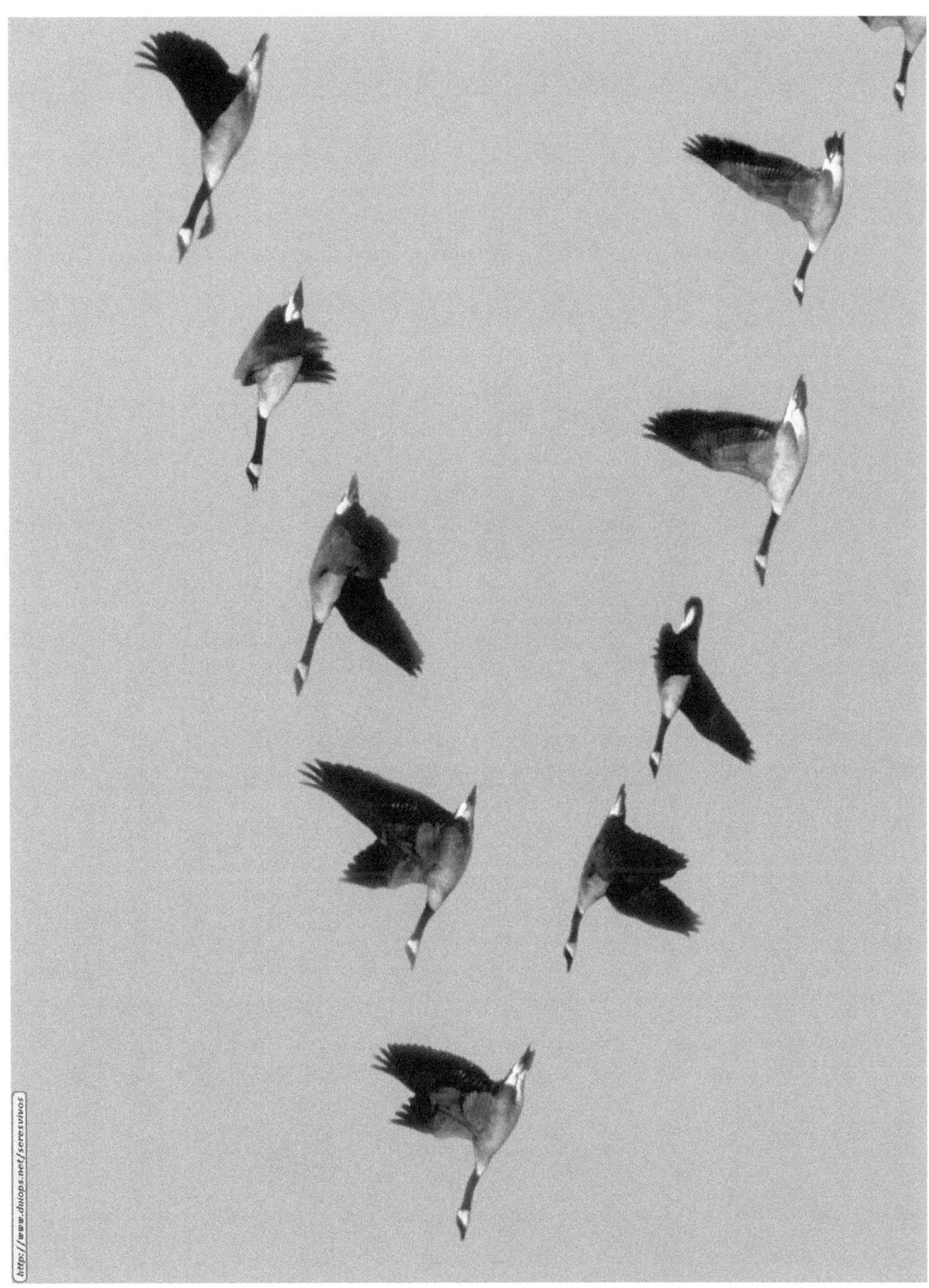

Image of Wall Sitting

Image of Wall Sitting

Bicycle Assembly Diagram

Bicycle Assembly Diagram

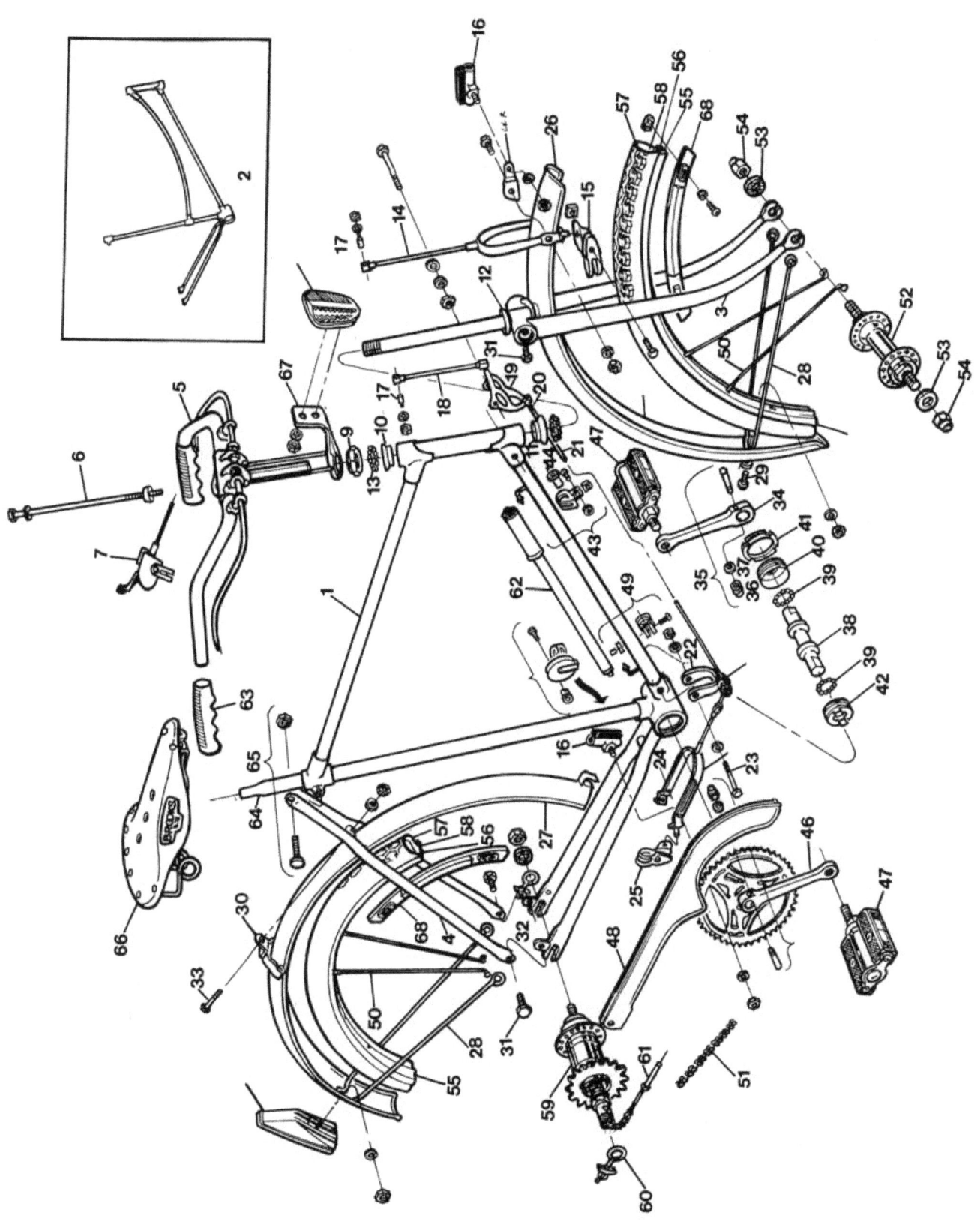

Bicycle Assembly Instructions

Bicycle Assembly Instructions

Official Rules: This is a nationwide marketing program with multiple locations throughout the United States and is invalid in any state where prohibited by law. We are delighted to provide anyone with a tour of our resort; however, only the individual(s) named herein are eligible to claim award items from this promotion. This promotion is designed to be of particular interest to persons who are between the ages of 25 and 70, with a minimum annual income of $40,000. **You must appear in person and present a written confirmed reservation in your name for a specific date and time to claim a prize.** Due to the value of this promotion you must present two forms of identification. This offer cannot be used in conjunction with any other Silverleaf Resorts offer. Pets are not allowed on tour. Silverleaf Resorts owners, employees and their immediate families, groups of two or more affiliated couples and persons who have toured our facilities within the last six months are ineligible for this offer. Please see the expiration date at the top of this notice. Any offers may be valid only on the day of the actual visit. **No purchase is necessary.** A purchase will not improve the chances of winning. After meeting the above listed criteria, you will receive an Instant Gold card at the resort, which will be your entry form. To be valid, you must scratch off any five squares in the presence of an authorized representative. If you reveal five (5) Pots of Gold, you are the instant winner of your choice of a new BMW X5, PORSCHE CAYENNE or MERCEDES-BENZ M-CLASS value $49,000 or $49,000 towards the purchase of the new vehicle(s) of your choice - current production models available in the continental US only) or $49,000 in CASH! Every Instant Gold card contains five Pots of Gold within the twenty-five (25) squares on the card. If you do not reveal the five Pots of Gold, compare the unique number printed on your Instant Gold card to the Official Awards List at the resort to determine your exact prize. The Instant Gold card is void if more than five squares are revealed in whole or in part. The odds for this promotion are: 1) The new vehicle, verifiable retail value $49,000 or $49,000 cash 1:53,130; 2) $1,500 Shopping Spree to Saks Fifth Avenue, Nordstrom, Macy's, Sears or Wal-Mart (or the store of your choice), verifiable retail value $1,500, 10:53,130; 3) Exotic five-day, four-night Island Getaway to your choice of Aruba, Hawaii (Oahu or Maui), Jamaica or Puerto Rico, average verifiable retail value $806. **Voucher must be registered within 60 days and allows one full year to select and complete travel. You must pay a $30 refundable deposit prior to making a reservation.** Certain blackout dates apply for some destinations. Reservations are subject to availability and some restrictions may apply. **Travelers must be 21 years of age and are responsible for any applicable local, state or federal taxes as well as airfare, transportation, gratuities, meals and incidentals** 53,059:53,130; 4) $500 Cash, 20:53,130. Silverleaf Resorts guarantees the following minimum number of awards: (a) one (1) new vehicle, verifiable retail value $49,000 or $49,000 cash (the winning participant must choose either a vehicle or the cash award); (b) ten (10) $1,500 Shopping Sprees to Saks Fifth Avenue, Nordstrom, Macy's, Sears or Wal-Mart (or the store of your choice), verifiable retail value $1,500, and (c) twenty (20) $500 cash awards (the minimum guarantee). The promotion starts on April 1, 2013. It ends when either 53,130 Instant Gold cards have been distributed, or the new vehicle, verifiable retail value $49,000 or $49,000 in cash, or ten (10) $1,500 Shopping Sprees, or twenty (20) $500 cash prizes have been awarded, or on March 31, 2014, whichever occurs earlier. No later than sixty (60) days after the promotion has ended, any unclaimed major awards to be awarded under the minimum guarantee for this promotion will be awarded through a random drawing from the names of participants. The drawing will take place at the office of the sponsor. All qualified participants receiving an Instant Gold card prior to the end of the contest will be included. Winners agree that their names and/or photographs may be used for future promotions without further compensation. Winners will be notified by phone or mail. The Bonus Gift Certificate is valid only if a 90-minute sales presentation at a Silverleaf resort has been completed before redemption. Married couples must complete the presentation together. Due to the value of this gift, you must present a valid driver's license and a major credit card. At the time of gifting you will be asked to choose from one of the two bonus gift options, approximate retail value $795. The Las Vegas/Orlando vacation voucher is redeemable for two round-trip airfares and two night's accommodations. **Voucher must be registered within 120 days and allows one full year to select and complete travel. You must pay a $100 refundable deposit prior to making a reservation.** Flights depart midweek from major airports in Atlanta, Austin, Boston, Chicago,

Official Rules: This is a nationwide marketing program with multiple locations throughout the United States and is invalid in any state where prohibited by law. We are delighted to provide anyone with a tour of our resort; however, only the individual(s) named herein are eligible to claim award items from this promotion. This promotion is designed to be of particular interest to persons who are between the ages of 25 and 70, with a minimum annual income of $40,000. **You must appear in person and present a written confirmed reservation in your name for a specific date and time to claim a prize.** Due to the value of this promotion you must present two forms of identification. This offer cannot be used in conjunction with any other Silverleaf Resorts offer. Pets are not allowed on tour. Silverleaf Resorts owners, employees and their immediate families, groups of two or more affiliated couples and persons who have toured our facilities within the last six months are ineligible for this offer. Please see the expiration date at the top of this notice. Any offers may be valid only on the day of the actual visit. **No purchase is necessary.** A purchase will not improve the chances of winning. After meeting the above listed criteria, you will receive an Instant Gold card at the resort, which will be your entry form. To be valid, you must scratch off any five squares in the presence of an authorized representative. If you reveal five (5) Pots of Gold, you are the instant winner of your choice of a new BMW X5, PORSCHE CAYENNE or MERCEDES-BENZ M-CLASS value $49,000 or $49,000 towards the purchase of the new vehicle(s) of your choice - current production models available in the continental US only) or $49,000 in CASH! Every Instant Gold card contains five Pots of Gold within the twenty-five (25) squares on the card. If you do not reveal the five Pots of Gold, compare the unique number printed on your Instant Gold card to the Official Awards List at the resort to determine your exact prize. The Instant Gold card is void if more than five squares are revealed in whole or in part. The odds for this promotion are: 1) The new vehicle, verifiable retail value $49,000 or $49,000 cash 1:53,130; 2) $1,500 Shopping Spree to Saks Fifth Avenue, Nordstrom, Macy's, Sears or Wal-Mart (or the store of your choice), verifiable retail value $1,500, 10:53,130; 3) Exotic five-day, four-night Island Getaway to your choice of Aruba, Hawaii (Oahu or Maui), Jamaica or Puerto Rico, average verifiable retail value $806. **Voucher must be registered within 60 days and allows one full year to select and complete travel. You must pay a $30 refundable deposit prior to making a reservation.** Certain blackout dates apply for some destinations. Reservations are subject to availability and some restrictions may apply. **Travelers must be 21 years of age and are responsible for any applicable local, state or federal taxes as well as airfare, transportation, gratuities, meals and incidentals** 53,059:53,130; 4) $500 Cash, 20:53,130. Silverleaf Resorts guarantees the following minimum number of awards: (a) one (1) new vehicle, verifiable retail value $49,000 or $49,000 cash (the winning participant must choose either a vehicle or the cash award); (b) ten (10) $1,500 Shopping Sprees to Saks Fifth Avenue, Nordstrom, Macy's, Sears or Wal-Mart (or the store of your choice), verifiable retail value $1,500, and (c) twenty (20) $500 cash awards (the minimum guarantee). The promotion starts on April 1, 2013. It ends when either 53,130 Instant Gold cards have been distributed, or the new vehicle, verifiable retail value $49,000 or $49,000 in cash, or ten (10) $1,500 Shopping Sprees, or twenty (20) $500 cash prizes have been awarded, or on March 31, 2014, whichever occurs earlier. No later than sixty (60) days after the promotion has ended, any unclaimed major awards to be awarded under the minimum guarantee for this promotion will be awarded through a random drawing from the names of participants. The drawing will take place at the

Virtuous Circles Diagram

Virtuous Circles Diagram

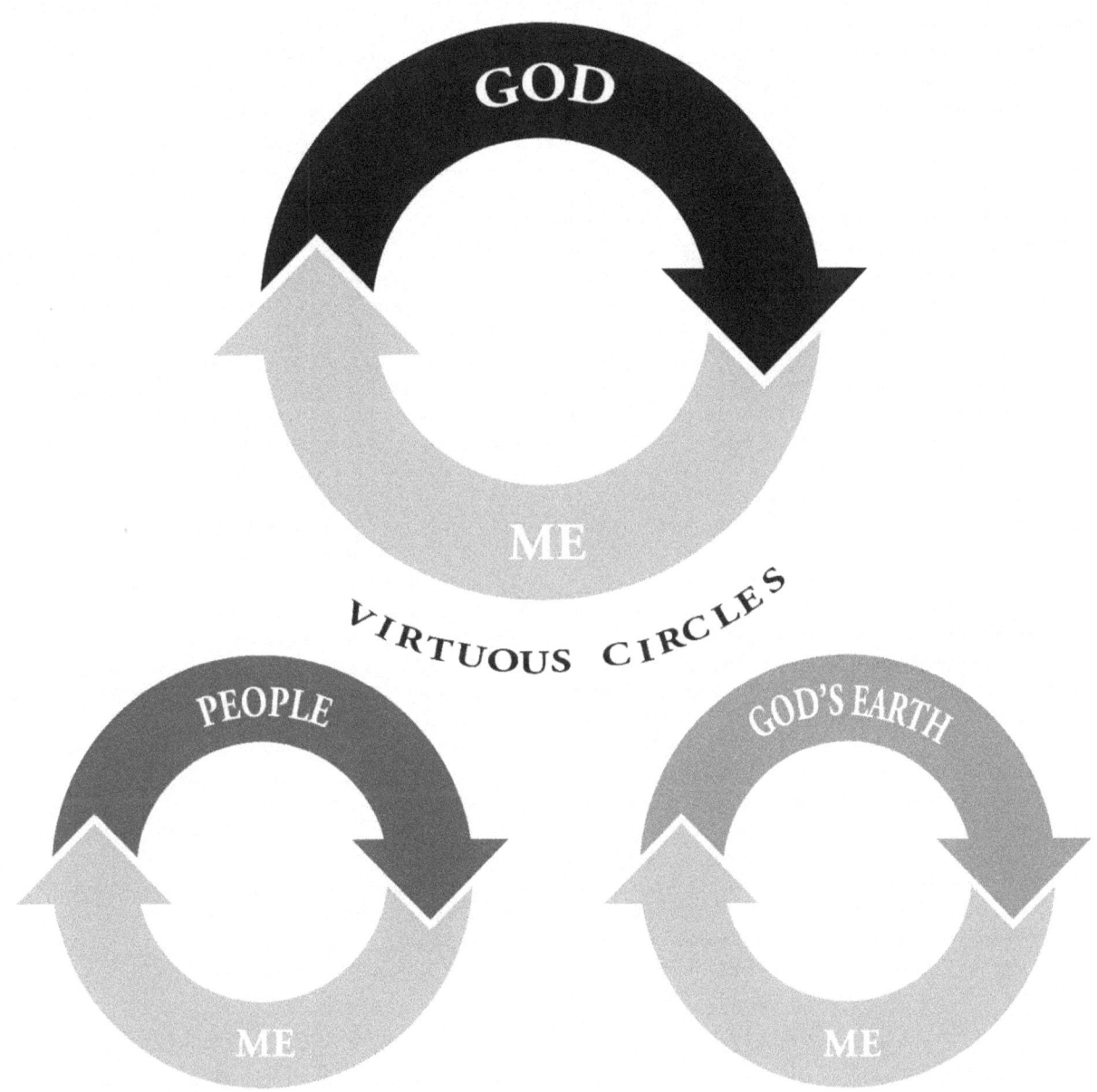

Presentation Feedback Form

PRESENTATION FEEDBACK FORM

Creating Jobs ACADEMY

Speaker: _____

Topic: _____

Directions: Please provide comments and circle actions the speaker did well.

	KEYS TO ENGAGE THE AUDIENCE	POSITIVES	AREAS FOR IMPROVEMENT
TOLD STORIES	Used personal stories, Used stories of others, Illustrated the topic well.		
EXPRESSED ENERGY	Moved among audience, Varied voice volume, Maintained eye contact, Used gestures effectively, Said or did something unexpected, Was warm and positive.		
SHOWED VULNERABILITY	Shared own mistakes/struggles, Used self-depracating humor, Expressed empathy/solidarity, Acknowledged audience expertise, Expressed gratitude.		
CREATED INTERACTION	Asked open-ended questions, Gave time to think about questions, Listened well, Referred back to audience input, Invited input from those who hadn't spoken, Broke into pairs, trios, or groups.		
USED VISUALS	Used flipchart/whiteboard, Used visually powerful slides, Illustrated with a physical object, Used pictures or audio/video recordings.		
MANAGED CONTENT	Was true to curriculum, Expressed enthusiasm for the topic, Communicated clearly, Ended on time.		

Contributors

Evan Keller, Lead Author & General Editor – Above all, Evan is a follower of Jesus. His daily goals are to: learn, create, relate, move, give and thank. Karen is his beloved wife of 29 years. Evan is a University of Central Florida graduate, an ordained minister, a member of: Rotary, NAACP, Volusia Remembers Coalition, and Christ Community Church in Daytona Beach, as well as a frequent visitor at Greater Union First Baptist Church (a 140-year-old African American congregation). Evan is passionate about nurturing trusting friendships and healing across the color line. As a founder of Beloved Communities Inc, he finds great joy in friendship with brothers and sisters of color in which he sees unique aspects of God's image and who model character traits of perseverance, courage, and forbearance. Evan is addicted to playing basketball, and uses off-road biking, paddling, and mountain backpacking to deepen friendships and soak in the beauty of God's Creation. He enjoys crossing cultures, art, the blues, and books on theology, nutrition, business, and African-American history. Speaking of books, he is also the lead author of StartBook, GrowBook, The Heart of Wealth, and I, the Lord, Love Justice. At work, Evan co-leads talented teams at two ventures he founded to leverage business for good: the nonprofit Creating Jobs Inc (creatingjobs.org) and the for-profit Tree Work Now Inc (treeworknow.com). Through God's grace and creative teamwork, these two ventures are exemplifying the true purpose of business to "serve by creating value." Together, they advance Evan's vocational purpose to "co-create thriving businesses and communities."

Candice L. Davis, Co-Author – Candice crafted the fictional narratives in Course Two and provided general editorial assistance for both courses. As the founder and CEO of Go Write Something, Candice L. Davis helps entrepreneurs write books to increase visibility and profitability. Candice is passionate about and committed to making business ownership accessible to the people who can most benefit from it. Candice lives in Atlanta, GA, with her wonderful husband and is the mother of two brilliant daughters and grandmother of one perfect granddaughter.

Jeff Hostetter, Co-Author – Jeff co-created the 12 habits with Evan and was a helpful sounding board throughout the curriculum development. He has been happily married to Diane for 31 years! They live in Lancaster, PA and have two children: Adam (25 and married) and Kelly (18). Jeff enjoys: a relationship with Jesus, eating ultra-healthy, riding his electric bike, serving as a small group leader and elder with his church family, and a warm relationship with Compassion International. Jeff is a board member and Director of Partner Relations for Creating Jobs Inc. He is co-founder and former CEO of Elexio Church Software, current business partner with TGF Medical Software, and leader of a local chapter of Christian Business Fellowship.

Dr. Andres Panasiuk – Thank you for your encouragement, mentorship, and insight into how youth learn and how partner organizations prefer courses be formatted. Your intimate knowledge of Latin American culture was helpful at several key points. We also appreciate your edits to the 12 truths.

Nazrine-N Navetia, Compiler & Formatter – Thanks for cheerfully digitizing Evan's handwritten "chicken scratch" and for working on formatting and publishing issues. Nazrine Nadhezdah Navetia is a daughter of the King, Yahshua born to serve by affirming and bestowing hope to others. She enjoys the gifts of two sons Dae-Malyk (23 yrs.) and Channan-Kai (10 yrs.) and is grateful for her life partner Troy David. She enjoys her dog Chi-Chi (shy-chee) and her cat Catori as well as her variety of plants. She studied legal assisting at the associate level, attesting to her passion for justice. Her study and practice of corporate and personal finance, both professionally and personally has proven to be both excitingly challenging and enlightening. Nazrine practices reading, writing, thinking and acting as daily habits. She serves her community as an Outings Leader and ExCom member with the Sierra Club.

Carol Keller-Vlangas, Proof-reader – Thank you for proof-reading the manuscript. Carol utilized her experience as an English teacher and career educator who has invested in thousands of new entrepreneurs over the years, including her son Evan!

Karen Obuhanych – Thank you for allowing us to use your perfectly fitting "Under the Mango Tree" painting for our front cover art (used with permission via licensing agreement). See more of Karen's work at www.ktoart.com.

Tom & Carroll Keen – Thank you for hospitality! Evan's two weeks of writing at your serene and cozy mountain cabin was essential to the creation of this curriculum. You share in all the good fruit this will bear.

www.ingramcontent.com/pod-product-compliance
Lightning Source LLC
Chambersburg PA
CBHW081209170426
43198CB00018B/2896